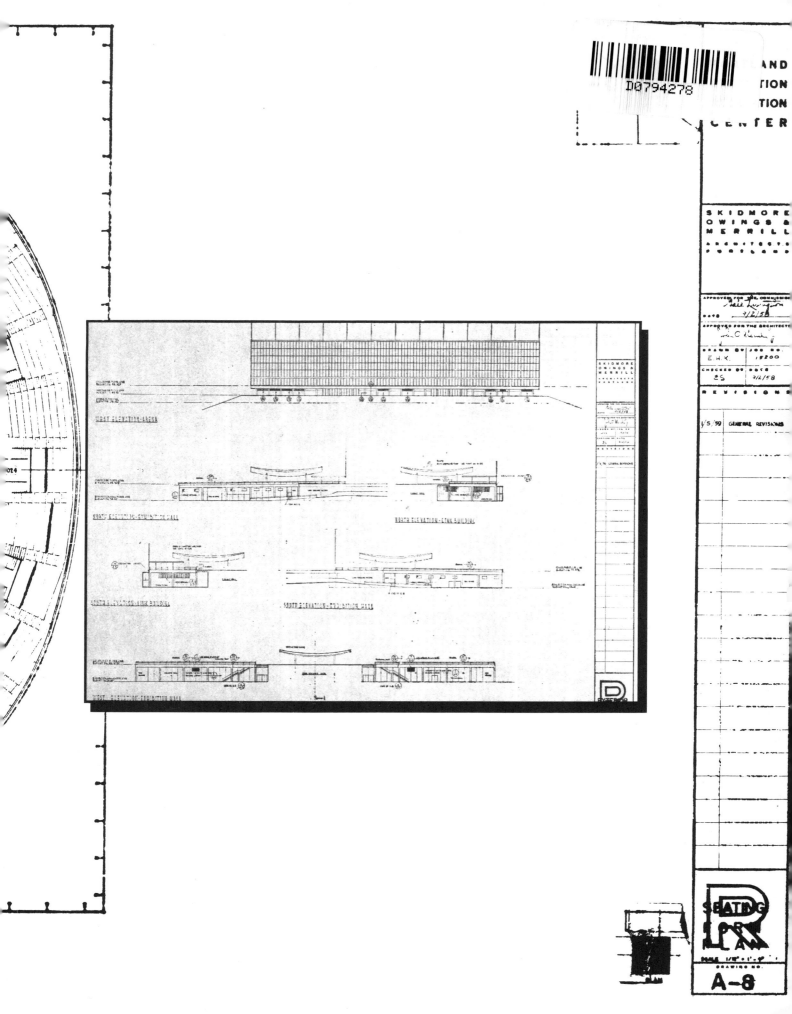

AND
TION
TION
CENTER

SKIDMORE
OWINGS &
MERRILL
ARCHITECTS
PORTLAND

WEST ELEVATION-ARENA

NORTH ELEVATION-EXHIBITION HALL

NORTH ELEVATION-LINK BUILDING

SOUTH ELEVATION-LINK BUILDING

SOUTH ELEVATION-EXHIBITION HALL

WEST ELEVATION-EXHIBITION HALL

SEATING PLAN

A-8

RIP CITY!

A Quarter Century with the Portland Trail Blazers

STEVE CAMERON

For those patient sports editors and assorted other bosses who put up with all my crazy notions and
let me keep on learning — but especially for good old boy Bob Hentzen in Topeka
and one tough German, Bick Lucas, who caught a few bullets himself. — Steve Cameron

Steve Cameron has been covering pro basketball and assorted other sports as a newspaper reporter
and columnist for more than two decades. Winner of numerous awards for overall sports writing and
works on subjects as varied as greyhound racing and basketball on the Navajo reservation,
Cameron also edited *A Golf Guide to the Caribbean* which was published in 1983.

Cameron is the author of six sports-oriented books, including a 75th-anniversary commemorative
on the Green Bay Packers and *Last of a Breed,* a biography of baseball legend George Brett.
Cameron's account of a cross-country rail trip, *Last Train to America,*
will be released by Taylor Publishing Company in 1995.

Now a full-time author and radio commentator, Cameron lives in Kansas City.

TAYLOR PUBLISHING COMPANY
Jack Smith   Publisher
Bob Snodgrass   Publishing Consultant

TD MEDIA, INC. PACKAGING

PORTLAND TRAIL BLAZERS
Chuck Charnquist   Coordinator

ROBERT ENGLE DESIGN

TRAIL BLAZERS 25TH ANNIVERSARY BOOK COMMITTEE
Sharon Higdon, Jim Taylor, Heather Corcoran, Pat Lafferty, Linda Temple,
Angela Dean, John Lashway, Marta Monetti, Eric Charnquist and Tia Hughes

FIBER OPTICS PHOTO: Wolf Photography and Chris Dennis

DUST JACKET DESIGN: Roger Greiner

Rose Quarter rendering in gatefold courtesy of Art Zendarski Architectural Illustration, San Francisco, Calif.

Aerial photo of Rose Garden construction courtesy of Skyview Aerial Surveys, Eugene, Ore.

Endsheet Rose Garden Drawings courtesy of Ellerbe Becket Architecture.

Endsheet Memorial Coliseum Drawings courtesy of Skidmore, Owings and Merrill Architects.

Contributing Photographers: Gary Akiyama, Gary Allen, Owen Carey, Gordon Clark, Brian Drake, Bill Gillingham, Don Grayston,
Max Gutierrez, Albert Hall, Dave Hatheway, Roger Jensen, Jim Lund, Michael Mathers, Jay McAlonen, Greg Mirecki, Dave Olson,
Ralph Perry, Brett Patterson, Paul Schroeder.

Remaining photography courtesy Portland Trail Blazers and NBA Photos.

Special archival photo assistance by The Oregonian Publishing Co., Serge McCabe, Director of Photography, and Margie Ramirez,
Photography Research and Sales.

Contributing Photographers *The Oregonian:* Claudia Howell, Michael Lloyd, Dale Swanson, Jim Vincent, Randy Wood.

Published by Taylor Publishing Company,
Dallas, Texas

ISBN: 0-87833-089-5 (General)
ISBN: 0-87833-090-9 (Limited)
ISBN: 0-87833-091-7 (Collectors)

CONTENTS

ACKNOWLEDGEMENTS

*A*sk an author what it's like to write a book and most will say: "Fun, but hard."

Some stories obviously are tougher to wrestle into manuscript form than others — which, of course, makes the job harder, but surely more challenging. This tale of the remarkable Portland Trail Blazers, and the place they occupy in the very soul of Oregon, ranked right up there in degree of difficulty.

Oh, the people involved were wonderful, and everyone from top to bottom in the Blazers organization — past and present — were almost unfailingly cooperative. Ditto the fans, media witnesses and others in the NBA community who gave freely of their time and memories to help make RIP CITY! a book worthy of this 25-year celebration.

But yes, it was hard.

Through sheer happenstance, we were hustling things into the final stages when the Blazers went through major management and coaching changes. There was much rushing around and hurry-up phone calls fairly sizzled in an effort to make the book as complete and up-to-date as possible.

We did our best, and yet all of it could have turned to ashes without some yeoman help from a few special members of the Blazers crew. Chuck Charnquist, that lovable fellow you've seen at the Coliseum press table all these years, was designated as the club's point man for the book project. Well, Chuck delivered above and beyond the call of duty. Maybe they should retire his Blazers sweater and hang it up there with Bill Walton's jersey number.

Thanks, also, to John Lashway and John Christensen, those public relations whizzes who kept stitching things back together. And, of course, to everyone on the 25th anniversary committee — Sharon Higdon, Pat Lafferty, Jim Taylor, Heather Corcoran, Angela Dean, Linda Temple, Tia Hughes and any others I've inadvertently missed. That breakfast was a special treat, gang.

There is no way to list everyone I talked to while trying to put the whole Blazers story in perspective, but some people gave extra time and effort, sitting still for fairly lengthy interviews when they surely had other things to do. That blessed group included Harry Glickman, Paul Allen, Larry Weinberg, Marshall Glickman, Geoff Petrie, Bill Schonely, Jack Ramsay, Rick Adelman, Clyde Drexler, Don McClave, Bucky Buckwalter, Bill Walton, and, an old pal of mine, former *Oregonian* columnist Terry Frei — hats off, T-Bone, for those lessons on Portland geography.

I've drawn on countless newspaper and magazine articles, as well. There's no way to identify them all, but thanks to the reporters and authors who told Blazers stories so that I might retell them later. And, by the way, this project might never have been finished without those magnificent scrapbooks put together so lovingly over the years by Sister Maxine Currin.

I'm also grateful for information gleaned from several books about the Blazers: *Promoter Ain't A Dirty Word*, by Harry Glickman; *The Coach's Art*, by Jack Ramsay with John Strawn; *The Breaks of the Game*, by David Halberstam; *Against the World*, by Kerry Eggers and Dwight Jaynes; *The Long, Hot Winter*, by Rick Adelman with Dwight Jaynes; and *Nothing But Net*, by Bill Walton with Gene Wojciechowski.

Some people quite important to the Blazers story also deserve a deep bow for taking the time to contribute special sections of this book in their own words: Harry Glickman, Jack Ramsay and Portland journalism legend George Pasero.

This is getting to be a pleasant habit, but another round of applause, please, for everybody at Taylor Publishing Company — especially Bob Snodgrass, Jack Smith and Arnie Hanson, who are helping pay for those guys landscaping my yard. Thanks to Tony Seidl's design group and Frank Coffey for his scrupulous editing job. Don't blame Frank if you find a mistake — it's mine. And hey, for Jamie Montgomery and Kim Shannon down at the office, lunch is on me just for your patience.

Special mention for April Hall, who guards my cats with her life so I can roam off to Portland and other points of the compass; for superstar travel agent Becky Carpenter, who can get you from here to Bangladesh and back over the weekend; for the whole crew at the Best Bet in Beaverton, who made those trips a barrel of laughs; for Susan Pierson, who works for Paul Allen and set a world record for faxes trying to steer me into Bellevue for my appointment; and certainly to my Kansas City buddies Gib Twyman, Jeff Flanagan and Tim Keithley, just for hanging out at the track or taking my phone calls when it was time for serious whining.

And finally, thanks to Foo's Custard for putting so much sugar in those sundaes that I never ran out of gas.

—**Steve Cameron**
Portland, Oregon
August 1994

FOREWORD

HARRY GLICKMAN, NOW PRESIDENT EMERITUS OF THE TRAIL BLAZERS,
WAS THE MAN WHO BROUGHT THE FRANCHISE TO PORTLAND IN 1970 AND HAS GUIDED THE TEAM
IN SEVERAL CAPACITIES TOWARD ITS CURRENT STATUS AS ONE OF THE JEWELS IN ALL
PROFESSIONAL SPORTS. A NATIVE OF PORTLAND WHO WAS A SUCCESSFUL SPORTS PROMOTER
EVEN BEFORE LANDING THE NBA TEAM AFTER A 15-YEAR EFFORT,
GLICKMAN WAS ELECTED TO THE OREGON SPORTS HALL OF FAME IN 1986
AND WAS NAMED PORTLAND'S FIRST CITIZEN IN 1993.

I've always been amazed how seemingly insignificant things sometimes can have such a profound affect on major events.

It's no exaggeration to say that, if not for a misplaced raincoat, Portland would not have been awarded a National Basketball Association franchise in 1970. And of course, I wouldn't be writing this foreword for a commemorative book.

But happily for everyone, we got our team and now it's time for a book that can capture — both in words and pictures — the quarter-century history of the Trail Blazers. We hope it will become a treasured possession for many of our fans.

Let me begin by reconstructing some of the events that led to Portland joining professional sports' big leagues. Back in 1954, following a campaign called, "Big League or Sad Sack City," voters approved funds for the construction of a new coliseum — along with other expenditures, including remodeling our zoo. Once that issue passed, I immediately began seeking an NBA franchise.

At that time, the league had only nine teams and was based almost exclusively in the East. Commissioner Maurice Podoloff's mentality was, more or less, that anything west of Brooklyn was foreign territory.

But in the 1960s, under new commissioner Walter Kennedy, the NBA embarked on an aggressive expansion campaign that put teams in Phoenix, San Diego and Seattle. The Lakers and Warriors already had moved to Los Angeles and San Francisco, so the West was open. From our standpoint, all these cities were natural rivals of Portland from our days in baseball's old Pacific Coast League and the Western Hockey League.

I had known Kennedy from his days running the New York office of the Harlem Globetrotters, so we had a friend on our side when we applied for a franchise.

Our original intention was to put together a local group and then conduct a public stock offering, but that plan fell through when we couldn't obtain interim financing. And the truth is that I was getting desperate by the time the NBA Board of Governors scheduled a meeting for Feb. 5, 1970 in Los Angeles.

Dick Vertlieb, the former general manager of the SuperSonics, called about that time to say that someone in Seattle might be interested in a Portland franchise. I invited Dick to bring the gentleman to Portland, and you can imagine my surprise when the man turned out to be Herman Sarkowsky — my wife's former brother-in-law.

Herman let us know he wasn't keen on any interim financing arrangement, but that he'd be interested in buying the franchise if he could get two other partners involved. As it turned out, I was leaving the next day to meet the league's expansion committee in Los Angeles. So Herman told me he'd try to get in touch with his prospective partners and he'd phone me when he heard from them.

The bottom line, though, was that I didn't have much to work with at the expansion meeting, which was held in the hotel suite of Washington Bullets owner Abe Pollin. I hadn't heard from Herman, so I presented my plan for a public stock offering — and was promptly told that somebody would have to come up with a substantial part of the down payment on the $3.7 million expansion price.

I left Abe's suite, heading for my own hotel and some bad-news calls to the investors back in Portland. But then I remembered that I'd left my raincoat in Abe's bedroom — and when I went to retrieve it, Sarkowsky called. He told me that his partners, Larry Weinberg and Bob Schmertz, were prepared to jump in and buy the franchise.

That misplaced raincoat and subsequent telephone call changed the history of sports in Oregon forever.

I returned to the expansion meeting and told everyone that I had solid investors who were ready to put up the entire purchase price. What we needed, they said, was a letter of credit for $750,000 that had to be presented to a governors' meeting by noon the next day.

Sarkowsky made arrangements with his bank in Tacoma for a sister bank to issue me the letter of credit. But that bank was located in downtown Los Angeles, and when I went to pick up the precious letter the following morning, I ran into a monumental traffic jam. I

Harry Glickman and his wife, Joanne, have been cheering the team on for a quarter century.

finally retrieved the letter and raced to the meeting, which was being held at the offices of the National General Corporation.

When I didn't arrive on time, Pollin excused himself to go to the bathroom and remained there until I came dashing in 20 minutes late. I've often kidded Abe that it was the longest bathroom visit on record.

Along with representatives from Cleveland and Buffalo, we were told to return to the meeting at 3 p.m., when we'd be informed of the league's decision. When I got back, along with Nick Mileti from Cleveland, Ray Patterson told us to look surprised when the commissioner appeared, but that we were now members of the NBA.

By the time I got back to my hotel that day, the switchboard operator told me that I had received or placed more than 50 phone calls. I flew back to Portland that evening and held a press conference the following Saturday morning. On the plane ride home, I'd compiled a list of about 300 things that had to be done — most of them immediately and some of them yesterday.

The college draft was only six weeks away, and we needed a scout desperately. An old friend from the San Francisco 49ers, Art Johnson, rang to recommend Stu Inman. Talk about moving quickly: I got in touch with Stu, who flew to Portland the same afternoon, took the job after an hour meeting at the airport and zoomed off to Salt Lake City on his first scouting assignment.

Our first draft choice and the first Trail Blazer player turned out to be Geoff Petrie, who shared Rookie of the Year honors with Boston's Dave Cowens. Stu did an outstanding job as our director of player personnel.

One of the most fortunate choices I made from that infamous list of 300 things to do was the selection of our radio announcer. I found out from Bill McFarland, president of the Western Hockey League, that Bill Schonely might be available. I'd known Bill as the voice of the Seattle Totems in the WHL, and soon enough we offered him the job. What a pick: Bill has become the most visible and even revered member of the organization. He introduced the now-famous phrase, "Rip City," which has become a nearly universal reference to the Trail Blazers.

On the court, we naturally suffered through the pains of expansion. Under coach Rolland Todd, we won 29 games in our first season — the second-best record of any expansion club in league history.

I'm amused by people who tell me they've been fans of the Trail Blazers from day one. We sold only 1,100 season tickets our first year. One of the highlights was when we beat the New York Knicks — defending NBA champs — 114-96 on Jan. 9, 1971 in front of the largest crowd of the season, 11,808. While Blazermania didn't become part of our vocabulary until we won the championship in 1977, I'll always believe it started with that first team.

I'm extremely proud of the Trail Blazers' accomplishments in our first quarter-century.

Winning it all in 1977, of course, was the most thrilling event in our history. No one in the organization — players, coaches, staff members — ever will forget that moment or the subsequent outpouring of pride and affection it produced. We still get excited at the memory of that wonderful parade and celebration at Terry Schrunk Plaza the day after our clinching victory.

One of my proudest possessions is a letter I received from Walter Kennedy's secretary after his death in 1977. It was the last letter he dictated before he died. She sent it to me unsigned.

Kennedy's letter read, in part: "Only you and I are left who remember the hammers of hell that you went through to get the financing the very night before the Portland franchise was granted in Los Angeles on that famous occasion. It seems like yesterday!

"Harry, you above all deserve great credit for Portland winning the NBA title. Your patience and perseverance and creation of a great front office were the key elements in what ultimately was a victory on the court of play. Without the other, there would be no championship."

Those words mean so much to me.

It is generally agreed in the industry that the Trail Blazers are one of the model franchises, not only in the NBA, but in all professional sports. The Trail Blazers introduced in-house radio and television, were the first to show games on closed-circuit television and experiment with cable TV. The marketing department is second to none, and one of the comments which makes me most proud came from commissioner David Stern: "The first thing I tell an expansion franchise is to go visit Portland."

Of all the records the Trail Blazers have established, the one which makes me proudest is our 769 consecutive capacity crowds, the longest streak of sellouts going on anywhere in the sports world. This incredible support from our fans has more than justified my belief that Portland belongs in the major leagues.

The Trail Blazers have become the most visible institution in Oregon and have brought national and international recognition to our city and state.

We've always attempted to be good corporate citizens, and our commitment to charitable and civic causes is second to none. Last year alone, for example, the Trail Blazers — players and staff —were involved in 740 worthwhile causes.

When we started this team a quarter-century ago, we had a staff of 10. Today that number is 160 and will continue to grow as we prepare to move into our new state-of-the-art arena. The Rose Garden will be the finest facility that modern technology can design and construct anywhere in the world. I believe the next 25 years will bring even more enjoyment and entertainment to our fans and that the NBA, currently the best league in all of professional sports, will become even better.

Whenever I get upset because I can't find something, I always think back to that misplaced raincoat. It was one of the luckiest things that ever happened to me — and, I hope, for all Trail Blazers fans.

INTRODUCTION

DR. JACK RAMSAY, WHO LONG HAS BEEN REGARDED AS ONE OF THE MOST KNOWLEDGEABLE
MEN IN BASKETBALL, COACHED THE PORTLAND TRAIL BLAZERS FROM THE
1976-77 THROUGH 1985-86 SEASONS, AND REMAINS THE BLAZERS' WINNINGEST COACH WITH 453
VICTORIES. HE LED PORTLAND TO ITS ONLY NBA TITLE IN 1977. RAMSAY, A MEMBER
OF THE NATIONAL BASKETBALL HALL OF FAME, ALSO ENJOYED A SUCCESSFUL COLLEGIATE COACHING
CAREER AT ST. JOSEPH'S (PA), AND COACHED BUFFALO AND INDIANA IN THE PRO RANKS.
HE IS CURRENTLY AN ANALYST ON NBA TELECASTS.

*I*n December of 1970, I was coach of the Philadelphia 76ers, flying
to Portland to play the Blazers in their inaugural season. What struck
me most vividly as we approached the airport was the grandeur of
Mount Hood, arrayed in a mantle of pure white, appearing to be a
massive sentinel over the area.

The next impression was the deep green hue of the landscape that
blanketed the countryside below, contrasted against the brown ribbon
of muddy water that was the Columbia River. I remember thinking:
How green it is down there, and this is mid-winter.

Then later, walking without a topcoat with a couple of Philly writers
along those clean downtown streets from hotel to restaurant,
breathing the fresh air, I can recall saying, "This looks like a nice place
to live." Of course, I never dreamed that it would happen.

And when it did, when I later became coach of the Trail Blazers and
my family settled in Lake Oswego, I looked forward to early morning
runs along the Willamette River — catching glimpses of Mount
Hood on clear days as the sun rose over its shoulder, turning the color
of white snow to pastel hues of pink, purple and orange.

Back to that first trip to Portland — I remember the game so well,
and perhaps so do a lot of Blazers fans. It's hard to forget the long one-
second count at the end of regulation time that enabled Sixers guard
Archie Clark to tie the score. Clark took an inbounds pass, faked his
man, dribbled, then fired in a long jumper — somehow before that
one tiny second had ticked off the clock. My Sixers went on to win in
overtime. When you're the visiting coach, you're just happy for any

kind of break, but I did feel a tug of empathy for Blazers coach Rolland Todd.

Even in the early years of the Portland franchise, it was evident that Blazers fans were special — strong and loud in support of their team, but also appreciative of an opponent's good play. It was impressive, just like the landscape.

A few seasons later, when I was coaching Buffalo, Bill Walton agreed to be a guest on my radio program prior to a Braves-Blazers game in Portland. Bill was in his second NBA season and we talked about how different the pro game was from college basketball, and about the special role that a dominant center plays. Such programs last only a few minutes, but I recall how easy it was to talk with Bill, how much ground we covered and how we seemed to agree on the various points we discussed. As the interview ended, I thought how great it would be to coach a player like Bill Walton.

The following spring, I got that chance. Stu Inman called to tell me that the Blazers were going to make a coaching change and asked if I might be interested. I was, mostly because of the potential of a team with a player like Walton.

Once I was hired, I was immediately impressed with the sense of "family" in the Portland organization. Owner Larry Weinberg was deeply involved, but had business concerns in Los Angeles. He appeared to have great confidence in a small staff to run the operation. There was Harry (Glickman), Stu (Inman), George (Rickles), Berlyn (Hodges), Wally (Scales) and John (White). And an office force of Sandy (Sedillo), Gail (Miller), Mary (Conchuratt) and Meredith (Wayt). It sounds strange in the big-business context of sports today, but that was the whole group — efficient, warm and friendly, and they made a newcomer feel welcome.

My first task was to meet with each player to tell him about the kind of game we would play and what his individual role appeared to be. I learned a lot from these personal contacts with the players and their families.

I recall the meeting with Walton most vividly of all. As we finished our discussion, I got up to leave, but Bill said, "Coach, there's one more thing."

And what might that be, I wondered.

"Don't assume we know anything," he said.

My feet hardly hit the pavement as I walked to my car. I knew that if a team's best player had that mindset, we were going to have a great team.

That same time period coincided with the NBA college draft. My evaluation of our club to Blazers management had been that there was not enough speed at the guard positions to play the up-tempo game I wanted. Inman agreed with my assessment, but he really liked Wally Walker, a small forward from Virginia, as our No. 1 pick. He felt that Dave Twardzik, coming to us from the now-defunct ABA, would add speed to the guard corps; further, that fleet-footed Johnny Davis, a guard from Dayton, would be available when Portland got around to using our two second-round picks.

On draft day, we got Walker as planned in the first round, and when our turn came to pick in the second, Davis was still there. But Inman took Major Jones, a big forward from Albany State. He looked over at me, silently shushed my look of dismay, then selected Davis with the other

Jack Ramsay takes the microphone in a January 14, 1993, pre-game ceremony in which Blazers uniform No. 77, symbolic of the 1977 championship, is retired in his honor. During the ceremonies, Ramsay was added to the Blazers' Walk of Fame in Memorial Coliseum, joining Harry Glickman, Larry Weinberg, Geoff Petrie, Maurice Lucas and Bill Walton.

Ramsay on patrol.

second-round pick two slots later. We got the player we wanted, but not before my sweat glands had been thoroughly activated.

There were a few common threads that bound the 1976-77 Blazers into a tightly knit unit. They were all essentially team players who were more focused on group success rather than compiling personal statistics. They were all good passers, a rare trait among NBA teams. And most had experienced the misery of losing, and were anxious to do whatever it took to win.

At the beginning of the season, we played great at home and terribly on the road. We didn't win a road game until December. But whenever we got back to our home court, there was an immediate transformation. There was something about playing in front of those loyal Blazers fans packed in the close confines of Memorial Coliseum. It seemed like all Oregonians were Blazers. We were them and they were us.

Eventually, of course, we began to win on the road, too, and we were playing outstanding basketball heading into the playoffs. But the Blazers were not very good in the first two games of the Finals — nervous and tight in Game One, sluggish and unfocused in Game Two. So we were down 0-2 to a very good Philadelphia club. It was as if we suddenly realized we were playing for the NBA championship and wondered if we really deserved to be there.

Late in the second game, Sixers center Darryl Dawkins took a punch at our forward, Bobby Gross. The nimble Gross ducked and the blow opened a cut under the eye of Dawkins' teammate, Doug Collins. Then, before order was restored, Maurice Lucas went after Dawkins, landing a looping right behind Darryl's ear. The two squared off, both benches emptied and people streamed onto the floor, ready to swing at anything in a red uniform. There were no serious injuries, although my assistant coach, Jack McKinney, later told me, "I got one fan real good."

That turned out to be our last really tough time in the Finals.

We had played so badly in Game Two that Sixers star Julius Erving said, "Portland needs some new plays. They do the same thing all the time." But that wasn't it. On the long flight home, McKinney and I conferred and decided not to change anything. No new plays, no tinkering. We just had to get back to playing our game.

And we did.

Remember the last few seconds of our series-clinching victory in the sixth game, when the Sixers took a couple of shots that could have tied the game? Walton finally batted a rebound to Davis — the guy I was sweating out on draft day — and we were world champions.

The scoreboard kept flashing the same message: "NBA CHAMPS!" Players and coaches exulted, and fans crushed together on the floor. The locker room was a wild scene filled with squirting champagne, hugs and handshakes. Everyone was wrapped up in the moment except backup center Robin Jones, who sat in a corner by himself — angry because he hadn't played in the game.

I'll never forget that parade the next day, riding in an open

Ramsay was a passionate leader and teacher.

convertible with my wife, Jean, and my daughter, Carolyn. I looked up and waved to an older gent, who smiled down at us, his face framed in the window of a dingy rooming house somewhere between the railroad station and Broadway. I wonder yet: Did he know what it was all about?

Then the caravan turned onto Broadway and was forced to inch along through a wall-to-wall mass of people. They were jammed across the wide street. Some got above the crowd and dangled from light poles, while others leaned out office windows. They were all expressing sheer joy that their team had won. It was a stunning spectacle.

Did that all happen yesterday, or was it 17 years ago?

The next season, the Blazers were even better — through 60 games, of which we won 50. That was truly a great team and such fun to work with. I enjoyed every minute we were together. The players were so in tune, they reacted in complete harmony to each movement of a teammate or an opponent. We were just running through the entire league.

Then came the injuries to Walton, Lloyd Neal, Gross and Twardzik. And as quickly as the team had come together, it came apart.

Walton went through a messy legal suit, and although he played later with the Clippers and Celtics, he never performed again with the same excellence. Neal retired. Gross, Twardzik and Steele played on, but needed the others to be at their best. Lucas and Hollins became disgruntled with their contracts and were traded. Herm Gilliam was waived to make room for rookie T.R. Dunn. Davis, Jones, Walker and Corky Calhoun were traded in an effort to find suitable replacements for the others.

A great team, scattered to the winds. It was sad.

The remainder of my tenure with the Blazers was spent trying to get back to the top. There were good players — Mychal Thompson, Calvin Natt, Kenny Carr and Kermit Washington; Sam Bowie, Jim Paxson, Darnell Valentine and Fat Lever; Kiki Vandeweghe, Clyde Drexler, Terry Porter and Jerome Kersey. But there were never enough of them together to win another championship.

Coach Rick Adelman's Blazers later came close to winning a title twice, getting to the Finals in 1990 against Detroit and again against Chicago in 1992.

Both those seasons ended with heart-rending losses for the Blazers. When you're personally involved, no words can assuage the pain of defeat. Away from the scene, one can admire the fierce effort, the togetherness and the iron resolve that goes into a near-miss. But when you're on the inside, I can tell you, it hurts.

Now the torch has been passed once again. Adelman and former general manager Geoff Petrie leave the Blazers organization knowing that their jobs were well done. Bob Whitsitt and P.J. Carlesimo take on the challenge of putting together and coaching the Blazers back to the top of an extremely competitive league. There are important player personnel and coaching decisions to be made as the team equips itself for another run at the top.

The Blazers these days are a hugely staffed big business, and continue to expand their fiscal horizons. Soon they'll leave Memorial Coliseum and all its memories to play in a magnificent new building.

But some things in Portland will never change. Mount Hood maintains its constant vigil. The air remains clear and clean. And the salmon still swim upstream to spawn. Retired Blazers continue their lives and raise families — more than a few right there in Oregon.

And Blazers fans? They're still the best.

—**Jack Ramsay**
Ocean City, New Jersey
July 1994

Jack Ramsay's intensity is captured on the sidelines.

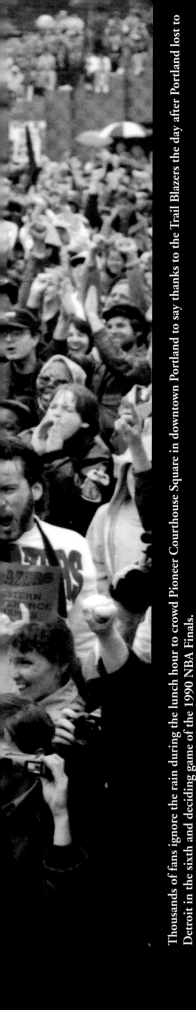

A New Name For The Rose City

"*P*ORTLAND DOESN'T HAVE AN EIFFEL TOWER OR A GOLDEN GATE BRIDGE. WE HAVE THE TRAIL BLAZERS."
—CHAMBER OF COMMERCE PRESIDENT DON MCCLAVE

UNIQUE.

WHETHER THAT CHUNK OF THE WORLD BEYOND THE SHADOW OF MOUNT HOOD CARES TO ADMIT IT OR NOT, HERE'S A SIMPLE TRUTH: THE PORTLAND TRAIL BLAZERS JUST AREN'T LIKE ANY OTHER NBA FRANCHISE. IN FACT, YOU'D BE HARD PRESSED TO FIND A CLOSE COUSIN ANYWHERE ELSE IN THE PRO SPORTS BUSINESS.

The differences involve all sorts of characteristics — geography, impact on the community, management which seems always to be plotting years ahead of the competition — but there is no doubt the Blazers occupy a singular spot on the athletic landscape.

"The thing that strikes you first is that there really is a love affair between the team and the people of Oregon," former Blazers hero Bill Walton said. "You hear other franchises and cities use words like that and claim to have deep emotion between teams and fans, but in Portland it's genuine. Blazers basketball is a perfect representation of the people in Oregon — rugged individualism blended with teamwork toward a common goal."

Bill Walton?

Isn't this the onetime mountain man and political gadfly who helped bring Portland its one glorious NBA championship, and then staggered locals by fleeing the organization in a wave of bitterness and accusations of medical messiness?

Indeed it is, but intervening years have given the redheaded giant some perspective.

"I've made a lot of mistakes in my life," Walton said, "but the biggest mistake I've ever made was leaving Portland. Honestly, I can look back now and feel incredible pride at being a Trail Blazer. To see my uniform number hanging in the rafters at the Coliseum gives me goose bumps every time I look up."

Walton is famous for speaking his mind, and sometimes tripping over his own opinions, but this time he's hit upon a piece of enduring reality. The relationship between the Blazers and their fans truly does resemble love — complete with moments of incredible joy, professions of loyalty, occasional bouts of hand-wringing concern and, yes, even full-fledged spats.

In Oregon, the populace cares. Deeply.

"This is probably the only team in basketball where 90 percent of the people in the state feel perfectly qualified to be coach or general manager of the Trail Blazers — or both," said broadcaster Bill Schonely, the club's voice since Day One. "Listen, I've been to just about every town and village across the state. Several times. And the one thing that just about everyone agrees about is how important the Blazers are to them. They don't always agree on what the Blazers ought to be doing or not doing at that moment, but these people are wrapped up in it."

Bill Walton is on hand when his No. 32 is retired on Nov. 3, 1989, the season's home opener that launched the club's 20th anniversary year.

The entire team returns to the floor for the post-game ceremony on Jan. 24, 1992, celebrating Bill Schonely's 2,000th game as the voice of the Portland Trail Blazers.

Oregon's corner-closet location on any U.S. map has something to do with the passion. So does the citizenry's rock-solid belief that no one outside the state's borders knows or cares what's going on inside.

Hall of Famer Jack Ramsay, who coached the Blazers for a decade and hauled the team to its greatest feat with the '77 title, recalled the reaction of friends and colleagues when he was considering the Portland job in 1976. Ramsay laughed, remembering how people back East actually would ask if the city was on the Canadian border. "They sounded like I was going off to Alaska," he said. "Nobody knew a thing about Portland except they'd heard there were a lot of trees."

And rain. Of course, the rain.

"The weather really is what most people in other parts of the country know about Portland," said Don McClave, who as president of the city's Chamber of Commerce was trying to explain what the Blazers mean to this community. "Here is this beautiful city, a wonderful place to live, a great place to visit and really an important commerce center. But for a long time, we suffered kind of a second-city syndrome because of Seattle. It was like the Northwest had this one great colossus up in Seattle, and everything else was forest. Here we are, happening to believe that the quality of life in Portland is better than anything in Seattle, but we were playing a part similar to Boston's relationship with New York.

"But then the Trail Blazers came along and Portland was in the big leagues. This is a true story: A few years ago, I was visiting Russia. We were in Kiev, and over there, far more young people speak English than their parents or grandparents. A lot of them get

Eight-time Blazers
all-star guard
Clyde Drexler
on one of his
familiar drives
to the hoop.

excited about seeing Americans and they want to try out some English. They're also big sports fans.

"We ran into some teenagers and they asked where I was from. When I told them it was Portland, they immediately lit up and one kid said, 'Portland? Trail Blazers! Bill Walton!'

"The relationship here between the team and Portland, and the team and the whole state of Oregon,

Owner Paul Allen is one of the yell leaders at a boisterous rally of Blazers fans who stood in the rain in Portland's downtown Pioneer Courthouse Square to cheer their team after it took Detroit to six games before losing out in the 1990 NBA Finals.

is just so much stronger than in most places. The Blazers have given us a stronger identity. And the result is that the basketball team is a regular topic of conversation on the street like nothing else since, oh, maybe the timber business in the old days. It's remarkable."

There's a lot of truth in this assertion from Pat Lafferty, who served the Blazers for several years on TV broadcasts and with the franchise's marketing arm: "Around here, even people who aren't particularly basketball fans keep up with the Blazers and follow the team pretty closely. They have to, just so they don't get lost in conversations at the office or over coffee. If you want to talk in just about any group at all, you'd better be able to talk about the Blazers."

Owner Paul Allen and Trail Blazers Vice Chairman Bert Kolde get into it in a big way from their end zone seats in Memorial Coliseum.

Consider one fine spring day just prior to the '94 playoffs, when a young man stood near the edge of a park in the Lloyd district. He was holding a sign that read: "Barging Kills Whales." Clearly, this fellow had higher planetary concerns than whether or not the Blazers could defend Houston's Hakeem Olajuwon. In

Former team owner Larry Weinberg remains a die-hard Blazers fan and frequently occupies a courtside seat, wearing his familiar red blazer.

fact, he offered up a brief little speech about how there were more important things in the world than basketball. But as his tiny audience of listeners began to drift away, the guy added, "And tell the Blazers that they'd better trade Drexler while he's still got some value."

That's Portland.

Owner Paul Allen knew before he bought this very special franchise that Blazers fans were involved. But as a Seattle native, he might have underestimated just a bit. Allen receives a constant outpouring of opinions from Blazers loyalists — by mail, through talk-show forums and even in person at Memorial Coliseum. "People will walk right up and tell me what they think," Allen said. "Sometimes they're pretty blunt, but I like to describe it all as advice. Friendly advice."

Allen tossed out that last phrase with a big smile.

"I'm really a fan, just like everybody else in one respect," Allen said. "I want to win very badly. I get excited when we're playing well and I get down if we lose. The difference is that, since I own the team, sometimes I have to be careful about showing my emotions. You know, if we take a bad shot, maybe I'll wince like everyone in the building. Then I realize that there are thousands of people watching me wince. In Portland, every expression means something. The team is so important — to me and to them."

Proof? Try taking the population's pulse during a down time. For instance, check reactions to the Blazers' two-year mini-slide from Western Conference champions to their second straight first-round playoff exit in 1994. Street-corner conversations would make you wonder if the Blazers not only had slumped to playing terrible basketball, but that their once-rabid supporters were losing interest.

Remember now, the Blazers hadn't exactly turned into a doormat. They were wrapping up a 47-win season that would lead to their 17th playoff appearance in 18 years — and 12th straight, the longest active streak in the NBA. But in Oregon, expectations for the People's Team are always staggeringly high.

So on a sunny April afternoon up the Columbia River in The Dalles, waitresses at The Tapadera Inn waited for a big-screen telecast of that night's game and shook their heads. Nope, they said, the place wouldn't be full. Not like when the Blazers were winning. Not like the old days.

A shoe store clerk at the Lloyd Center mall in Portland had repeated the same mantra a day before. The Blazers just don't have it together right now, he lamented. Folks were down.

In fact, a smattering of boos actually had been heard at Memorial Coliseum. And booing the Blazers, even if it's sporadic and half-hearted, is huge news. Fan favorite Clifford Robinson, the man who made headbands a high fashion item in Portland, lashed out after one particularly frustrating defeat. Robinson chided the Coliseum audience for their few catcalls — which, when compared to things you hear in other arenas around the league, really was pretty tame fare.

The whole issue of Blazers fans raising their voices to

boo the home team, even occasionally, became such big news that the local media examined it with stories, studies, interviews and in-depth analysis. Their conclusion was that the Coliseum has been sold out so long with the same ticket-holders that the fans have become a little blasé about winning. They've begun to take it for granted.

Longtime star Clyde Drexler put an interesting spin on the rare bit of crowd razzing, though.

"Anybody who's played here can tell you we have the best fans in the league," Drexler said. "They've always been loud, supportive, loyal. They deserve championship-caliber basketball. But because they're into the team so much, they're also very knowledgeable. You can't fool 'em. I think the only time I've ever heard them get down on us is on nights when we haven't given the right amount of effort, or if we aren't playing smart. Really, if we come downcourt two or three times in a row and don't run the offense right, you start to hear some grumbling. I think they figure if they know how we're supposed to pass and screen, and where everybody's supposed to be, then we sure ought to know."

Lest outsiders get the wrong idea, however, don't think for a minute that the bloom is gone from the Blazers' flower. Blazers President Marshall Glickman, the man who oversees the club's business affairs, smiles at all these recitations from the past two seasons. He's heard it all before — sudden attacks of gloom and doom, and why can't we be back in the NBA Finals like we're supposed to be?

"Here's how bad it is," Glickman said with a chuckle. "Let's look at the bottom. Take the period from 1978 —

Geoff Petrie was Portland's first ever college draft choice

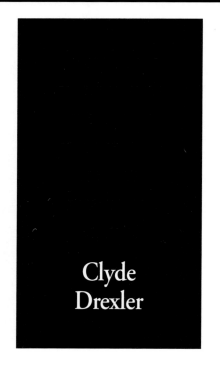

Clyde
Drexler

after we won the championship — to 1989. We were in the playoffs every year except one, but interest was considered low. This is a whole decade, and we didn't have one championship contender. Our TV ratings once got down to an 18.

"Pretty tough, right? Well, that 18 rating — our worst — was still the best in the NBA and it represented the second-highest number for any prime-time show, behind '60 Minutes.' And during that time, our waiting list for season tickets got longer.

"That was the bad time. There are an awful lot of teams that dream of having bad times like ours."

And why not? By any yardstick, the Blazers are a colossal success story.

On the court, they wrapped up a supposedly disappointing 1993-94 season with that 12th straight playoff appearance. Portland has missed postseason play just once since the Walton Gang won it all in 1976-77, and even then the club that missed (in '84) went 42-40. Since the expansion days of the early 1970s, the Blazers haven't ever really struggled. For instance, they've never had a lottery pick in the NBA draft.

Support? Well, those 769 consecutive sellouts at the Coliseum and construction noise from that state-of-the-art Rose Garden arena just up the street make a pretty compelling case.

"This situation is more like the loyalty you find for a college team, only here it's a professional franchise," former Blazers owner Larry Weinberg said. "It really is just like an extended family. Even the criticism is well-meaning. It's just that the Blazers mean so much to everybody in Oregon, expectations are always out of sight."

expectations and microscopic scrutiny.

"That's the way it ought to be," Walton said. "Playing great basketball and winning championships ought to be your goal. What's the point in being content with something less, with having something mediocre and acting like that's acceptable? The fans are right and the front office is right in shooting for the top. Every night, every season. People say, 'Well, be realistic. You can't win all the time.' And I say, 'Why not?' In Oregon, there's definitely a spirit of setting out to accomplish goals and then achieving them. It rubs off from the fans to the team. And that's just the way it should be."

"But I still love this team now just like the fans in Portland do. High expectations? You'd better have them in a major-league sport. Look at the other side of it: Would you rather have a team like the Clippers, who haven't had those kinds of expectations through the years? They haven't won anything, either."

Even Rick Adelman, the coach asked to step down in the spring of '94 despite five straight winning seasons with an average of 55 regular-season victories, professed no bitterness at the lofty standards which are so routinely demanded — and which cost him a job when

Coach Rick Adelman surrounded by the players he guided to the NBA Finals in 1990 and 1992.

Weinberg sold the club to Allen in 1988 but remains one of the Blazers' most incurable supporters. Part of the contract under which the franchise changed hands specifies that Weinberg always has a special phone line available so that he can ring up from anywhere in the world and hear the Blazers radio broadcast. "I've called to listen from New York, Washington, Romania, Israel, just about everywhere," Weinberg said. "Israel is about a nine- or 10-hour time difference, so my wife has told me from time to time that calling up to hear the games is just a little bit of insanity.

things turned just slightly stagnant.

"You have to look at it two ways, even if you're the guy on the spot," Adelman said. "Sure, you can get worn down by the expectations, because everybody's got an opinion. They want you to do something different, or play somebody else, or whatever. But that's because there's such a passion involved. And you can understand it. Our success made that happen. When you do something well — like the Blazers have for so many years — then you've set a standard that has to be matched or exceeded. It's tough, but it's a compliment,

Left: A youngster holds up a "Rip City" sign at a game in March of 1971. It was one of the first graphic evidences of what was to become Portland's basketball "name."

Inset: Broadcaster Bill Schonely, who coined the phrase, "Rip City," that became synonymous with Portland Trail Blazers basketball.

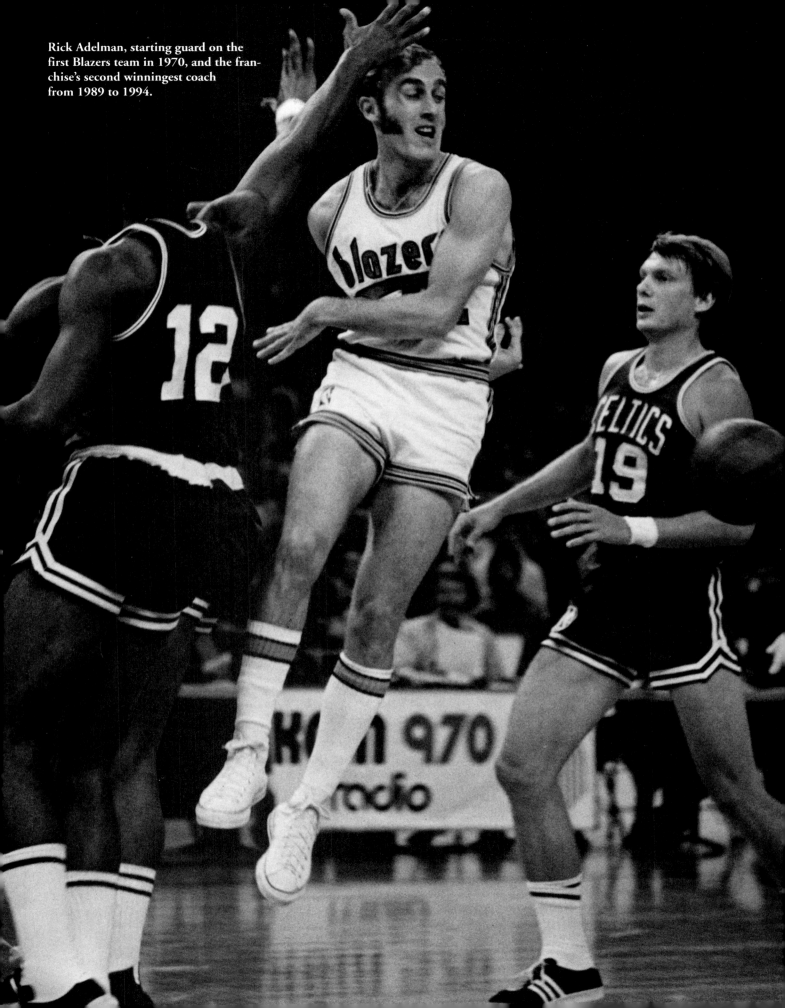

Rick Adelman, starting guard on the first Blazers team in 1970, and the franchise's second winningest coach from 1989 to 1994.

Byron Irvin, Jerome Kersey, Terry Porter and Clyde Drexler step out from under a protective awning to acknowledge cheers from fans at a 1990 rally in Pioneer Courthouse Square in downtown Portland.

Blazermania at its best.

too. You had to have the success in the first place to have all that pressure."

Adelman and Geoff Petrie, who resigned as Trail Blazers general manager following the 1993-94 season, have unique perspectives on the situation. They were not only teammates, but roomed together on the first Blazers team back in 1970. Adelman was the feisty point guard, Petrie a rookie scoring machine out of Princeton who wound up sharing NBA Rookie of the Year honors with Boston's Dave Cowens.

Adelman and Petrie both have insisted that Blazermania — that particular phrase popped up during the 1977 title year — actually started from the very first season. "You could tell the intensity and enthusiasm were there right at the beginning," Adelman said. "The only difference was there weren't as many fans at first, but the ones who came out were into it. And the numbers kept going up.

"The Blazers were important all over the state, too. I left the team (after three seasons), played a few more years in the league and then went back home to California to get into business. When I came back to Portland as an assistant coach for Jack Ramsay in 1983, my wife and I would be someplace in Oregon and we'd always be surprised when somebody would walk up and say hello because they recognized me. It's not like I was a big star or that I played on a championship team or anything like

Blazers broadcaster and marketing executive Pat Lafferty fires up a rally in Pioneer Courthouse Square in 1990.

Team founder Harry Glickman and his wife Joanne enjoy the action from their courtside seats.

that. But I'd been with the Blazers, and in Oregon, they're going to know you. It's really pretty amazing."

Petrie believes players and coaches go through a special experience in Portland.

"People here will wrap their arms around you," Petrie said. "Sure, they want to win and they've got plenty of opinions, but above all that they embrace the Blazers. There's a couple of things about that which really stick out. Look at how many guys who have played in Portland either stay here after their careers are over or come back later. And then look around the league through the years and see how many guys have played their best basketball here. There are very, very few players who have been better somewhere else than they have in Portland. Even with all the high expectations, this is just the perfect place to play pro basketball."

Jim Paxson was in his ninth year with the Blazers when he was traded to the Celtics mid-way through the 1987-88 season. Paxson had already decided that he loved Portland and intended to stay on, so after finishing up the season in Boston, he came back home.

"That summer when I got back, I was taking my sons to a Portland Timbers game," Paxson said. "Our tickets were at the will-call window, and there was an older lady working there who saw me and said, 'Jim, how nice to see you again.' I'd never met her before in my life. That's Portland."

A few things happened in the Blazers' first season that helped set the stage for the long-standing enthusiasm that now seems to have settled in for the duration. For one thing, a friendly schedule (heavily weighted with games against other expansion teams)

Blazers to the whole state, right from the beginning, and that has really paid off through the years.

"You can drive anywhere in Oregon now and see Blazers backboards, bumper stickers, schedules in windows, all of those things. Harry's philosophy got all that excitement going."

And then there was the magic moment that first year when the Blazers took on a permanent identity — a single phrase that has become the club's heart and soul, year-in and year-out.

Credit Schonely.

"Early in that first season, I was looking for a trade-

produced a surprising 29 victories.

But off the court, another dynamic was at work. The statewide loyalty the Blazers enjoy today — with its Blazer Cable TV network and the like — really took root because club president Harry Glickman decided early on that the franchise belonged to all of Oregon.

"As players, we used to gripe about this, but it turned out to be great for the franchise," Adelman said. "It seemed like we were always getting on a bus to go play a preseason game in Coos Bay or Pendleton or someplace else. The guys never enjoyed the bus rides or the little gyms, but Harry knew what he was doing. He gave the

mark call, something special that was all mine," said The Schonz. "A few things came and went, but nothing really stuck. Then one night we were playing the Lakers at home. There was a big, loud crowd because the Lakers were such a premier team — Los Angeles and all that — and the Blazers seemed to be able to raise their level for those kinds of situations.

"As it turned out, we got way, way behind. The Lakers were rolling along with a big lead and, all of a sudden, shots started falling and the Blazers are rallying and the place is jumping. Everybody's going crazy. We got within two points and had the ball — I'll never forget this — when

Harry Glickman waits at courtside to introduce new Blazers owner Paul Allen to the fans at the 1988-89 home opener.

Jim Barnett, a real character who'd been a hero at the University of Oregon, took a long jumper. He just swished the thing to tie the game and the Coliseum exploded. I hadn't even thought about this call before it happened, but the instant the ball hit the net, I hollered, 'Rip City!'

"I wish I could say I knew exactly what I was doing, the truth is that nothing about it was planned. I'd never even thought about that phrase before. But as soon as I said, 'Rip City,' some people with me there at the press table chimed in right away and said, 'That's good. You ought to leave that in your broadcasts.' So I did."

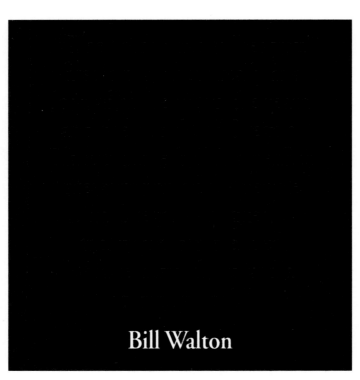

Bill Walton

And Rip City was born. There has been all sorts of discussion about how exactly Rip City should be defined. Is it a place, or a state of mind? Is it just a jumper from long range, or the spirit of the Portland Trail Blazers? No one has ever offered a definitive explanation, and that's been just fine, because Rip City eventually became an all-purpose rallying cry for Blazers loyalists.

As the franchise's successes have piled up and winning seasons stacked one upon the other, all those countless thrills throughout Oregon were — well, Rip City, baby.

And now, as the Trail Blazers celebrate a spectacular first quarter-century, a new era has begun. Personable, charismatic P.J. Carlesimo was coaxed away from a tremendously successful college program at Seton Hall to become the Blazers' eighth head coach. Carlesimo inherited a team with yearly championship aspirations in a state which remains ready to go crazy at a moment's notice.

Carlesimo is a very bright fellow who has never lived in the Northwest, but unlike the mystery surrounding Ramsay's move back in the 1970s, P.J. has arrived in big-time basketball country and knows it. "We're not rebuild-

Blazers broadcaster Bill Schonely interviews Blazers executive Marshall Glickman.

Clyde Drexler takes time to sign an autograph at courtside before the game.

ing here," Carlesimo said at his introductory press conference in Portland. "This is a situation where we're going to try to continue an excellent tradition and have 1977 all over again. We want to win another championship."

Good call.

Portland is very definitely among the NBA elite these days. The era once defined when New York Knicks boss Ned Irish groused that he couldn't sell many tickets putting the Portland Trail Blazers on the marquee at Madison Square Garden has long since become ancient history.

The Blazers made it to the NBA Finals twice in the 1990s and one season when they just missed — losing to the Lakers in '91 — they won 63 games in the regular season and may have been the best team in basketball.

The spotlight has found Portland, most definitely. The Olympic Dream Team began its 1992 run for the gold at the Tournament of the Americas in Memorial Coliseum. That same year, the NBA draft was held in Portland — the first time ever that event strayed from New York City. If only Ned Irish could have been around to see the furor in Rip City.

And now the finest arena in basketball is nearing completion.

"It's my dream come true," Harry Glickman said. "Portland has become big-time. For one specific thrill, I guess nothing can ever touch the championship of 1977, because that was something everyone in Oregon can cherish forever. But there's another kind of satisfaction in watching what's happened over the entire first 25 years. We've become one of the showpieces of basketball. You almost couldn't write a script any better than that."

No, you probably couldn't.

"This is probably the only team in basketball where 90 percent of the people in the state feel perfectly qualified to be coach or general manager of the Trail Blazers — or both."

Bill Schonely

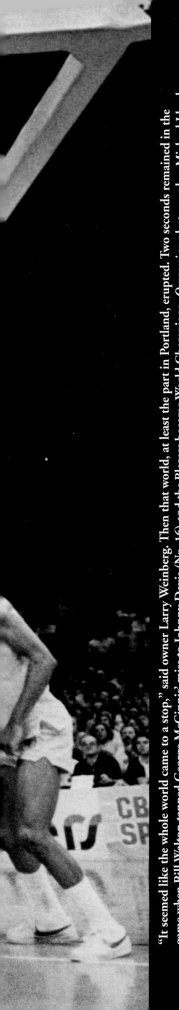

CHAPTER 2

ON TOP OF THE WORLD

"*W*HEN GEORGE MCGINNIS PUT THE BALL UP, IT SEEMED LIKE THE WHOLE WORLD CAME TO A STOP."

—LARRY WEINBERG

HAS ANYONE IN OREGON FORGOTTEN THAT SHOT?

HARDLY A SOUL.

IT HAPPENED, OF COURSE, ON WONDER SUNDAY — JUNE 5, 1977 — JUST SECONDS BEFORE THE TRAIL BLAZERS WON THEIR FIRST AND ONLY NBA CHAMPIONSHIP WITH A CHAOTIC 109-107 TRIUMPH OVER PHILADELPHIA IN THE JAM-PACKED, RED-HOT, SANITY-TAKES-A-HOLIDAY CAULDRON CALLED MEMORIAL COLISEUM.

That was the victory that sent a city and state into a collective frenzy. One woman fainted in the crush afterward but, as she was being lifted into an ambulance, the dazed lady managed to raise a hand and extend her index finger: We're No. 1!

There was pandemonium in downtown Portland, cars packed together in delirious, horn-honking gridlock. Laid-back Oregon, that sturdy but mentally cool corner of America, suddenly lost its mind with joy.

After six seasons of expansion frustration, the Blazers had erupted behind bearded giant Bill Walton and a remarkable cast of characters to reel off 49 wins in the regular season, then swamp the field in the franchise's first-ever playoffs. Crazier yet, they'd survived a talent-rich 76ers team in The Finals despite losing the first two games in Philadelphia — a feat accomplished only once previously in league history.

Yet the Blazers' fourth straight victory over Julius Erving, George McGinnis and the 76ers' assorted other bombers — the clincher that remains chiseled into Oregon sports history — was the most fantastic of all. For

one thing, it was the best game of the series, marvelous basketball at breakneck pace for the highest stakes.

And then there was the finish. Pulsating and poignant.

It hadn't seemed that the thing would hang on one bounce of the ball, not when the Blazers turned loose their hounding defense and precise, hurry-up passing game to rip off 40 points in the second quarter and lead 67-55 at halftime. The Sixers, who had been a disorganized and dispirited lot while frittering away Game Five back in Philly, appeared ready to collapse and let the celebration begin.

But that wouldn't have provided the proper drama.

Instead of politely fading away, the Sixers ignored the shooting woes of guards Doug Collins and Lloyd Free and climbed back into the fray. The sensational Erving — Dr. J of those many athletic gifts — poured in 40 points before the day was done and McGinnis, who had slumped the entire series, came alive with 28 of his own.

And suddenly the Blazers were clinging to a two-point lead in the final half-minute as the entire Coliseum went bonkers.

The crowd gasped in pain when star forward Bobby Gross was tied up with 16 seconds left and McGinnis won the tip, giving the Sixers a chance to knot the issue. Three chances, in fact.

"It was the kind of game I love most," Walton said later. "Two-point lead, final seconds, and the other team

with a shot to tie. The only thing that could have been better would have been if it had been a one-point lead. Just to make it more exciting." How much more could the fans have survived, Bill?

As it was, Erving launched one jumper that missed. Free collared that rebound, dribbled to the corner and tried to air-mail a jumper. All sorts of Blazers were flying at him, but it was the deceptively skilled Gross who blocked the shot out of bounds with five seconds remaining.

Now the Sixers were down to a final chance, and McGinnis was the man, collecting the inbounds pass and turning for a jumper in the lane. "I wanted the shot. It was a good shot," Big George said.

McGinnis had knocked in 12 of his 22 previous attempts, but this one was just a hair short with a tick or two left on the clock.

Blazers loyalists still see that ball in their dreams, watching it caroming loose to the mighty Walton, who instead of trying to clutch the rebound himself simply tapped it to guard Johnny Davis. And the clock — finally, blessedly — ran out.

In the bedlam that followed, something subtle and wonderful was temporarily overlooked. The Blazers, who had personified the team concept preached by Coach Jack Ramsay against Philadelphia's one-on-one superstar game, fittingly finished up with a play straight out of the Ramsay textbook.

When asked about that last rebound, Walton replied: "As a defender and rebounder, I don't think any shots are going in. If I can't get the rebound myself, I try to hit it out to the foul line. That's where our guards are supposed to be."

And where Davis was.

"I knew when I saw the ball come out there that I was going to get it and no one was going to get it from me," Davis said.

Here was everyone doing the right thing at the right time. Walton's by-the-book

Two Sixers superstars, Julius Erving and George McGinnis, were not enough to offset the balanced and determined Trail Blazers.

Johnny Davis dribbles to midcourt, referee Richie Powers signals it's all over, and a fan gives the victory sign as Oregonians start a celebration that lasts into the next day.

execution at crunch time was every bit as important as his game-long heroics: 20 points, 23 rebounds, 7 assists and 8 blocked shots. But that last move was Blazers basketball carried out to the final buzzer in the franchise's most historic game.

Perfect.

Actually, there was a bit of pixie dust sprinkled over the Blazers' entire season. It's almost impossible to imagine all the pieces which fell into place, setting up such a grand championship run.

Among other things, it took a merger of two leagues. The long-established NBA refused to use the M-word, instead calling it expansion rather than a merger when four teams from the exciting but financially doomed American Basketball Association — Denver, Indiana, the New York

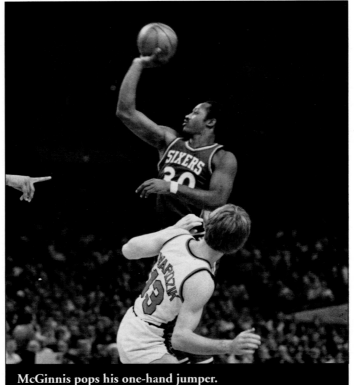

McGinnis pops his one-hand jumper.

Nets and San Antonio — were brought into the fold during the summer of 1976.

No one benefitted from the leagues' shotgun marriage in the short term as much as the Blazers, who had gone 37-45 the previous season. Portland promptly moved to shore up its backcourt in the off-season by signing a 1972 draft choice — tough, plucky Dave Twardzik — who had strayed off to become an ABA all-star at Virginia.

And that was just the start. The Blazers wanted even more from the dispersal draft in which the most worthy ABA players would be placed around the NBA. Portland had been just a little too good in 1975-76 to own a high enough choice in the dispersal sweepstakes, so general manager Harry Glickman and personnel

The signing of ABA all-star guard Dave Twardzik paid big dividends for Portland.

chief Stu Inman pulled the trigger on a controversial trade.

The Blazers' coveted power forward Maurice Lucas, whom Ramsay saw as the powerful enforcer he needed to complement Walton. So Portland packed off its best player of their first six seasons, popular and high-scoring guard Geoff Petrie, along with center Steve Hawes, in exchange for Atlanta's No. 2 choice in the ABA auction. Thus, after Chicago chose giant Artis Gilmore with the first pick, Portland jumped on Lucas.

It was certainly not a universally acclaimed move at the time. Petrie, who was Portland's first-ever draft choice in 1970, had averaged 21.8 points per game in his Blazers career (18.9 in 1975-76) and had proven himself a class act in every way. But the brass perceived, first, that Petrie would pose a contract problem if he stayed in Portland and, second, that the Blazers absolutely could not hope to contend for anything without an angry, bump-and-grind board menace like Lucas.

"(It) was something we literally didn't want to happen," Glickman recalled. "We were unable to sign Geoff Petrie to a new contract. We had been negotiating with Petrie and his agent, Larry Fleisher, for the better part of a year, but we finally reached an impasse. When it later became necessary to trade in order to obtain Atlanta's pick in the dispersal draft, the fact that we couldn't sign Petrie made it more palatable to involve him in a trade."

Another factor, especially on a team where some key players (Walton, Lloyd Neal) were physical question marks, was that Petrie needed knee surgery. However popular and productive Petrie had been, his health and contract problems made him expendable.

Ironically, the Blazers chose the same house-cleaning to unload the other half of their long-running, one-two scoring punch, forward Sidney Wicks. The talented but sometimes moody Wicks also had been beefing about money, and by the end of 1976, it was obvious that while the guy could score, Wicks just wasn't all that good for team chemistry. Besides, his scoring totals had declined — albeit slightly — in each of the four seasons since he rang up a 24.5 average as the NBA's Rookie of the Year in 1971-72.

Wicks didn't do himself any favors with Blazers management when Ramsay first arrived in town and set out to meet each of his returning players. Wicks gave the coach an earful of how much he was worth and even griped about the salaries paid to Ramsay and his predecessor, Lenny Wilkens. Wicks said out loud that the coach's dough probably ought to be his own.

From that point on, it was going to be: Good-bye, Sidney.

Actually, Wicks was peddled twice. The first deal, a straight sale to New Orleans, was voided by the Jazz. So at last, Wicks was purchased by Boston on Oct. 12. Just six days later, the Blazers made another tough transaction, trading away a promising young center they'd yanked from the dispersal draft, Moses Malone, for a future draft choice.

Glickman explained at the time that finances made it impossible to keep all his current players, plus newcomers Twardzik and Lucas, and still hang onto the promising but inexperienced Malone. The Blazers brain trust — most especially Ramsay and Inman — seemed to realize what Malone might mean to the future, but it was a trade that simply had to be made. One thing later softened the blow of losing Malone, who went on to become a perennial all-star: The 1978 draft choice Portland received for Malone at least turned into Mychal Thompson, who played 551 games and averaged 16.7 points over seven seasons with the Blazers before being dealt away for yet another useful center, former Oregon State hero Steve Johnson.

At one point, Glickman offered Wicks and Malone to the Celtics for guard Jo Jo White, but Boston guru Red

Future perennial NBA all-star Moses Malone was on the Trail Blazers roster when the 1976 fall camp opened but was traded before the start of the regular season in October.

Jack Ramsay

Auerbach finally decided that White — a key ingredient to a couple of NBA titles — ought to stay on in Boston. When that trade offer was rebuffed, the Blazers purchased the contract of guard Herm Gilliam from Seattle.

While all the preseason wheeling and dealing was going on, the 1976-77 Blazers also were adjusting to a new coach. Ramsay had been hired to replace Wilkens, another future Hall of Famer who had been downright unlucky and lasted just two seasons in Portland. Among the things on Walton's mind when training camp opened in 1976 was that his own fragility probably had cost Wilkens a job. A series of injuries had limited Walton to 35 and 51 games during his first two years, maladies that likely kept the Blazers from a trip or two to the playoffs.

"I really felt bad for Lenny," Walton said. "I felt responsible for him being fired. We were just starting to put things together and we obviously would have had better records my first two years if I'd been out there more. It was a blessing that I got to play for Jack Ramsay, who is absolutely a basketball genius, but the way things happened to Lenny at that time, it seemed kind of bittersweet."

Walton had come out of UCLA in 1974 as the best collegian in the land, and the Blazers got him with the No. 1 draft choice after winning a coin flip with Philadelphia. Those coin tosses were getting to be a way of life in Portland, and the '74 experience was the Blazers' first happy one. They chose a pleasant but physically limited center, LaRue Martin from Chicago Loyola, with the first pick in 1972 following contract squabbles with their intended selection, North Carolina's

Ramsay had at his side on the Blazers bench a very able assistant in Jack McKinney.

Bob McAdoo. Then they lost the flip in '73, when Collins went No. 1 to the Sixers. Portland eventually traded second choice Jim Brewer to Cleveland in a deal that proved less than useful to either side.

But the bottom line was that by '76, Walton was still in Portland, that he was healthy and still hungry as ever. There were worse alternatives, obviously: He could have been in Philly with Erving and McGinnis during the 1977 playoffs if the Sixers had called tails instead of heads. If he had been, the Sixers likely wouldn't have finished their season as beaten favorites in Portland. It's

almost inconceivable that there would have been a championship series in Portland at all.

So much for the ups and downs of the infamous coin flips.

As to the matter of Ramsay's arrival, there was good fortune involved in that, too. Ramsay had turned around a previously hapless Buffalo club and taken it to two straight playoff appearances. But Jack was available because he had become utterly disenchanted with Braves owner Paul Snyder and decided he had to leave.

"During the playoffs that final season in Buffalo,"

Maurice Lucas was a big-time rebounder.

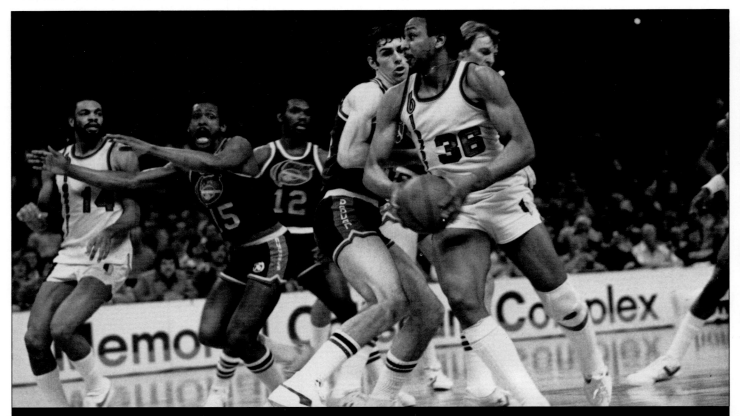

Lloyd Neal was tough, smart and invaluable.

Intensity personified:
Twardzik and Walton.

Corky Calhoun, solid and dependable, shows a perfect box out form.

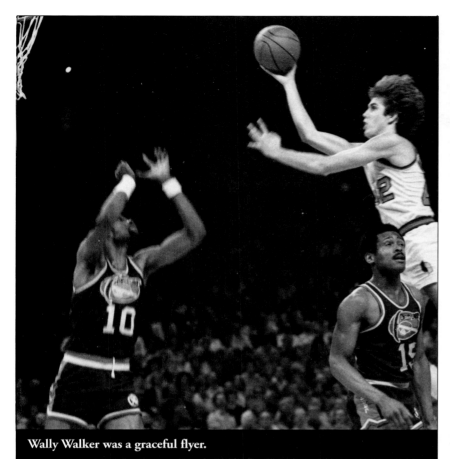

Wally Walker was a graceful flyer.

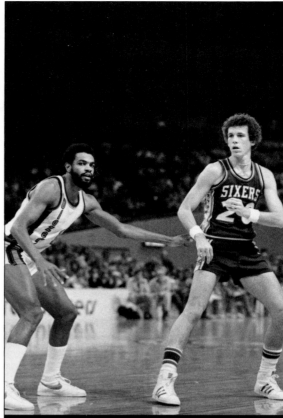

Lionel Hollins was the ultimate defender.

Robin Jones ably backed up Walton in 63 games.

Ramsay said, "Stu Inman called me from Portland. Would I be interested, Stu wondered, if the coaching job at Portland was available? My first thought was of Bill Walton. I really liked his game. I told Stu that I would be interested, and we arranged to meet in Buffalo. We talked theory, practice procedures, handling of players and many related basketball topics. I enjoyed the meeting and Stu told me he'd get back to me after the playoffs. My Buffalo team was eliminated by Boston, Snyder and I had our parting of the ways and I started to explore new coaching opportunities — but hoping the Portland job would materialize.

special. We had exactly the right mix to win." And Ramsay fearlessly trumpeted the news to an astonished media, predicting a playoff season for a franchise that had never so much as participated in a single playoff game.

Ramsay, though, smiled every time he looked down the roster and almost every time he conducted a practice. The revitalized Walton was a monster and brilliant creator in the middle, with Lucas and a very capable holdover, Lloyd Neal, providing muscle at power forward. Gross was perfect for Ramsay's running game at the small forward spot, and

Bobby Gross

Herm Gilliam

ize. Several weeks later, after meetings with Larry Weinberg, the team president, I agreed to take the job. The most enjoyable year in my coaching life was about to begin."

It all worked out providentially for the Blazers. By the time they opened the 1976-77 season, Ramsay had been installed on the bench (with a very able assistant, Jack McKinney, at his side) and was surrounded by the kind of players he loved to coach.

"Before we ever played a game," Ramsay said, "I realized that we had the makings of something very

the backcourt had gone from questionable to solid with Twardzik and Gilliam joining talented returnee Lionel Hollins and the lightning-quick Davis, who had been drafted out of Dayton. Robin Jones was the backup for Walton, and reliable, hard-nosed Larry Steele was still around for all sorts of tough assignments.

There was concern about Neal, who needed knee surgery, so Portland added another piece by signing defensive specialist Corky Calhoun off the waiver list.

Twardzik was the biggest surprise, and a delightful one. "Dave Twardzik's play was just superior to what I

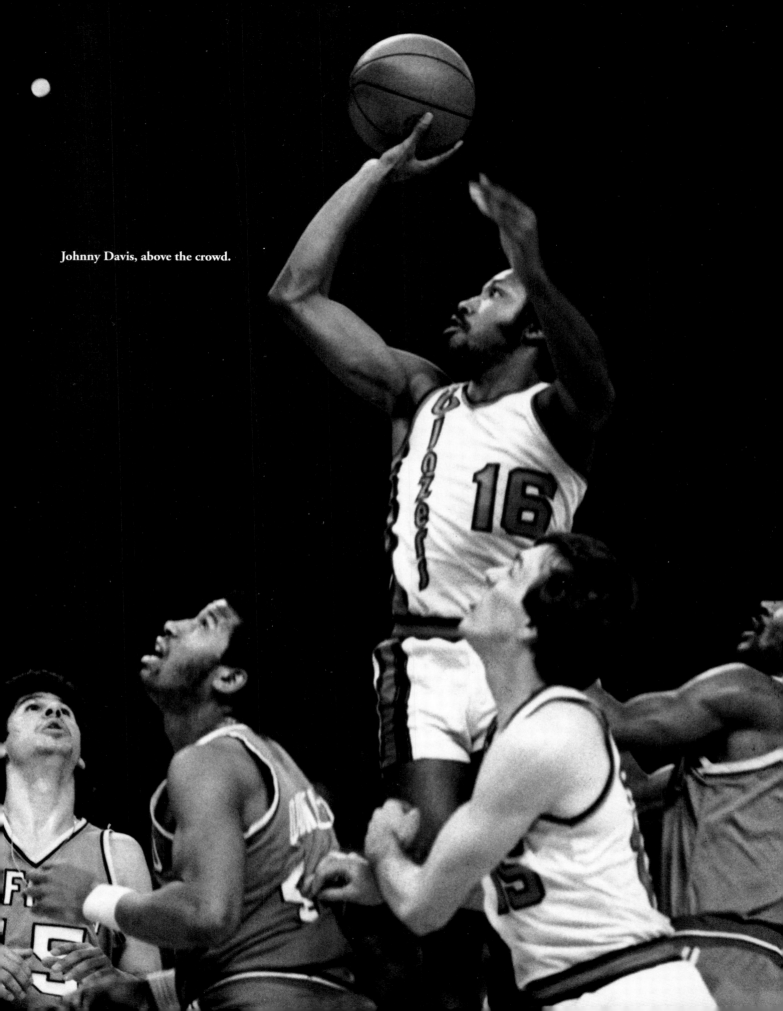

Johnny Davis, above the crowd.

expected, leading me to an adjustment in my plans for a starting lineup," Ramsay said. "I had initially considered using Hollins and Gilliam in the backcourt, with Davis and Twardzik as substitutes, but the combination of Twardzik's excellent play and a weakness in the ballhandling ability of a Hollins-Gilliam lineup persuaded me to start Dave along with Lionel.

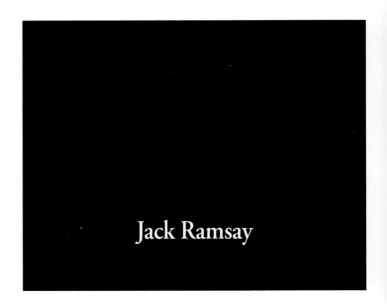

Jack Ramsay

"I didn't really appreciate Twardzik's overall skills until after training camp was underway. Despite Stu Inman's assurances to the contrary, I wasn't sure Dave was good enough to play very much for us. He doesn't look much like an NBA player. He's not very big, he doesn't have the speed of someone like Hollins or Davis and he can't really jump that high. All he does is whatever he has to do for the team to win. We were all astonished in training camp by Dave's ability to shoot a layup over the biggest players on the floor. He has a great first step to the basket and amazing control of his body in the air.

Lionel Hollins wears a face mask after suffering a depressed fracture in a game against New Orleans midway through the season. He missed six games before returning to action wearing this protective headgear.

Bill Walton, a brilliant creator in the middle, was perfect for Ramsay's running game.

A gathering of future Hall of Famers, with Dave Twardzik on the bottom of the pile. On top of him is Boston's John Havlicek, while Celtic center Dave Cowens and Bill Walton converge.

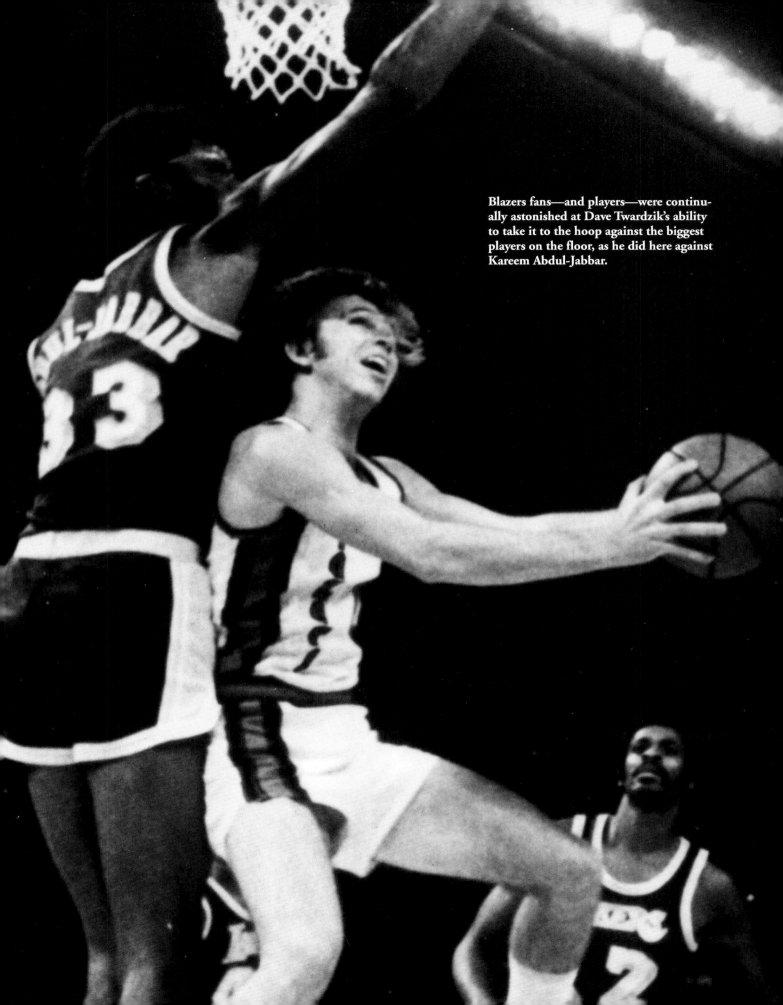

Blazers fans—and players—were continually astonished at Dave Twardzik's ability to take it to the hoop against the biggest players on the floor, as he did here against Kareem Abdul-Jabbar.

After a few days of swatting vainly at Twardzik's spinning shots off the backboard, Walton was reduced to laughter at his inability to block Dave's shot."

Camp wasn't all laughter, however.

Ramsay had given all his players a set of off-season

Matchups of premier centers — Bill Walton versus the Lakers' Kareem Abdul-Jabbar — were part of the glamour of the 1977 playoffs.

conditioning regimens and several other procedures he expected to be followed. Among the things Doctor Jack demanded was that everyone be on time. Well, training camp opened with a 7 p.m. meeting and three players were late: Walton arrived at 7:04, Gilliam and Lucas five minutes after that. As soon as trainer Ron Culp had passed out some introductory booklets, Ramsay calmly

announced that there was a $2-per-minute fine for tardiness. "That's $8 for you, Bill, and $18 apiece for Herm and Luke," Ramsay said, thus letting his promising young team know two things: One, that punctuality was demanded and, two, that no one would get preferential treatment.

Once the regular season started, the Blazers won seven of their first eight, thus serving notice to the league that something exciting might be happening out in the Northwest. And in early November, they put an exclamation point on that statement by destroying the 76ers 146-104 at the Coliseum.

"As I came on the court that night," Ramsay said, "I looked down to the end of the court where the 76ers were nonchalantly cruising through their warmups. I thought to myself as I went to our bench: They're not ready for us. And indeed they were not."

The blowout of Philadelphia's supposed super-team ended with the Coliseum crowd singing "Happy Birthday" to the surprised and delighted Walton, who was already sitting contentedly on the bench. It was a magical evening all around, and Ramsay remembered saying to himself afterward: "We could have beaten any team in the world tonight. I coach a team that could beat any team in the world."

Needless to say, things weren't always as easy as that rout of Philadelphia made it seem. The Blazers had a couple of serious problems to overcome before they could even be assured of a playoff spot, let alone contend for a championship: They had to learn to win on

Bill Walton

The Blazers-Bulls best-of-three series was hard fought all the way. Many considered it the toughest of all the tasks the Blazers had enroute to the 1977 title.

This crowd of 12,792 at an April 9, 1977 game against the Lakers was the second of what was to become an all-time professional sports record streak of consecutive sellouts. That number, including regular season and playoff games, reached 769 at the end of the 1994 playoffs.

the road, and they had to keep the brilliant but brittle Walton in one piece.

Ramsay was particularly distressed by his team's early woes away from home, especially since the same group ripped off a 15-game winning streak at the Coliseum without much trouble. The Blazers lost their first six on the road, continuing a trend from the bad old days that just had to be stopped. "The Trail Blazers over the years had developed a well-deserved reputation as a poor road team, creating a psychological hurdle we were having difficulty overcoming," the coach said. "We played without concentration or poise. Watching Jekyll play one night and Hyde the next was a puzzling and frustrating experience."

It was so vexing, in fact, that after a particularly sorry performance in Milwaukee—against a Bucks team that previously had lost nine straight—Ramsay just exploded. He ranted in the locker room, pounded the walls and eventually walked all the way back to the team's hotel without a coat in sub-freezing weather. Ramsay admitted

Denver, with such stars as Dan Issel (seen here battling Bill Walton), David Thompson and Bobby Jones, was a big challenge for the Blazers.

later that he was so angry, he never noticed the cold.

Perhaps the coach's eruption was a catalyst. Whatever, the Blazers promptly went to Indiana and stopped their road losing streak despite another average performance, then played an outstanding game to win at Phoenix. The corner had been turned.

Walton's health was another matter entirely. There was no doubting the big redhead's impact nor the rock-solid belief that this was a man who could lead a team to dreamy heights. Walton, though, managed to escape injury just once in his entire NBA career—and that was much, much later as a Boston reserve. Eventually his fragile underpinnings gave way during the Blazers' run to their first playoff appearance.

The inevitable injury came at a bad time, too. Walton was playing magnificently as the Blazers established themselves as one of the league's elite teams, beating both Boston and New York on the road, a Portland first. In one memorable victory at Chicago, Walton approached the bench while one of his teammates was shooting a free throw. "I'm hot as hell, but I can't get the ball," Walton told Ramsay, who immediately replied, "Don't worry, I'll get you the ball."

The Blazers then ran play after play to Walton, who scored every conceivable way over the 7-foot-2 Gilmore. When the game was over—Walton finished with 29 points—Bill simply grabbed the game ball and flung it high over his head in jubilation.

Another potentially troublesome injury came before anything befell Walton, as it turned out. The explosive Hollins suffered a depressed fracture after catching an elbow to the head in a game against New Orleans, so the Blazers knew for certain that they wouldn't get through the season on cruise control.

Then in mid-January, the Blazers tackled their toughest test of the year, an eight-game, 13-day road trip to several of the NBA's most inhospitable arenas. Even without Hollins, they struggled along on hard work and solid execution. Portland won three of its first seven on the trip before finishing with a stop in Denver.

It should have been a wonderful night. The Blazers erased a 19-point deficit against the best team that had come over from the ABA and won with several clutch plays down the stretch. Even by Ramsay's lofty standards, it was a superb performance, and the coach raced onto the court afterwards—first holding up his hand in a victory sign and grabbing the equally exuberant Walton. The game seemed to be such a watershed victory that Ramsay, McKinney and several other members of the Blazers traveling party went out late that night to celebrate.

The joy turned out to be short-lived. Walton woke up the next morning with soreness in his Achilles tendon, even though he couldn't remember having hurt himself in the game. Walton tried to play in the next game back in Portland, but he was in too much discomfort to be effective and, at last, the old bugaboo had struck. Walton missed the next 10 games and,

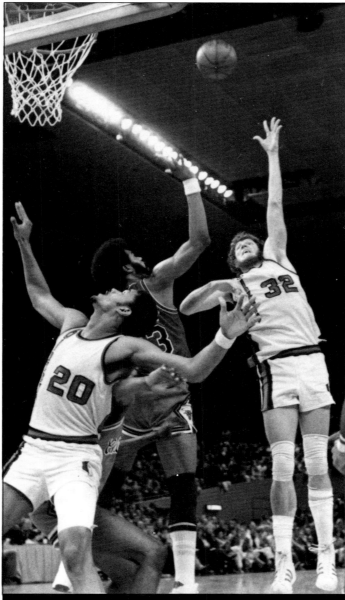

A battle of giants. Bill Walton and Chicago's Artis Gilmore go head-to-head in the key.

despite heroics and dogged play all around that left Ramsay pleased, the Blazers went 3-7. Jones simply couldn't live up to the full-time center's role, and Lucas wore himself to a frazzle trying to carry some of Walton's load along with his own. There was little doubt left that Walton would have to stay relatively injury-free if this was to be a fruitful season.

Walton returned to play about 20 minutes in a home-court victory over Boston—giving everyone a huge psychological lift—but then in March, in a game against the 76ers, Walton came down off-balance after snaring a rebound and sprained his ankle. Ramsay blamed himself, certain that he'd asked his star for too many minutes after that first long layoff. And to make matters even gloomier, the Blazers promptly lost four of the five games Walton missed while resting the ankle.

Later in March, though, everything fell back into place. Walton and Neal had recovered, along with Hollins. The Blazers began a rush, with no hope of catching the eventual division-winning Lakers but determined to hang on to a playoff position ahead of the Warriors.

Ramsay looked back on that stretch as the Blazers' most critical period of the year. And the most significant triumph of all came on March 17 at Oakland, when the old pro Steele scored a season-high 27 points in a crucial game that gave Portland a path to the playoffs from which they never strayed again.

By that time, fans back in Oregon had begun to catch the fever. Chants of "Playoffs!" rocked the

The scoreboard proclaims 'WE WIN' as the Blazers shake hands with the vanquished Bulls.

wins—very respectable, but good enough to earn them the home-court advantage for only the first-round war with Chicago. If a title was to be won, in other words, a lot of heavy lifting would have to be done far, far away from Memorial Coliseum.

Ironically, the Bulls provided perhaps the toughest test of the entire playoff run, and it was no surprise. Coach Ed Badger had rallied his team from a terrible start and the Bulls were on fire when the postseason rolled around, having won 20 of their final 24 regular-season games. Scarier yet, this was just a best-of-three format, allowing virtually no room for error.

The Blazers played their first-ever playoff game on April 12, and won it with the kind of team play Ramsay loved. They converted baskets off 28 assists to just 13 for the Bulls. Predictably, though, the Bulls bounced back to tie the series with a victory at home before a riotous crowd of 20,000-plus at Chicago Stadium.

Coliseum, and on April 5, a home game against Detroit drew a crowd of 12,359. And what was so special about that number? Well, it marked the last time the Blazers played to less than a sellout crowd before embarking on their incredible NBA-record streak of consecutive full houses. By the following summer, it was necessary to hold a drawing for the final 1,500 season tickets, and some games in 1977-78 were shown to cheering crowds on closed-circuit TV at the Paramount Theater.

There was still plenty of business to be done in '77, however. The Blazers would need victories in four playoff series to accomplish their Impossible Dream of winning a championship, and because of those early road problems and assorted injuries, they'd finished with just 49

Thus, the opening war came down to Game Three as Ramsay and others predicted it would. And it was a thriller. Portland led just 100-98 when Hollins, who hadn't been able to hit the broad side of a barn most of the night, tossed in a jumper from the top of the key just as the 24-second clock expired. Portland had survived the first round.

In the celebration afterward, Gilliam approached the grinning Ramsay and asked: "Coach, how come you picked Lionel to take that shot? He was only four for 15." Ramsay decided not to mention that the decision was made simpler because Walton, Lucas and Twardzik

Lionel Hollins led the Blazers backcourt. Inset: Herm Gilliam was sensational in Portland's Game Two win over the Lakers, 99-97, in the Forum.

Bill Walton's
slam-dunk over
Kareem Abdul-Jabbar
in Game Three of the
Western Conference
finals was one of the
magic moments of
the entire 1977 play-
off run.

Maurice Lucas "The Enforcer," prepares to fire an outlet pass.

had fouled out. Instead, he answered, "Herm, I knew he was going to make it."

With Chicago dispatched, the Blazers had to become poised, tough road warriors or face elimination. They were faced with the situation in subsequent series with Denver, Los Angeles and the 76ers where it was necessary to hold serve in every game at home and then find a way to steal at least one victory in hostile surroundings. A daunting task, indeed, particularly for a team that had been so road-shy just a few months previous.

But these were now mentally hardened Blazers, and they proved it immediately in the opener at Denver. The Nuggets were scary opponents, boasting a dangerous scoring trio of Dan Issel, David Thompson and Bobby Jones along with the distinct advantage of their mile-high home.

Nonetheless, Portland played Game One as though it could be life and death—as indeed it might have been. The issue came down to the final 20 seconds with the Blazers trailing by a point.

"During a timeout," Ramsay said, "I set up a play for us to run that called for a pass from Lucas to Gross at the top of the circle, followed by a backdoor play for Twardzik going to the basket. Denver had been overplaying on the weakside pass, a defensive strategy that I was certain would give Dave an opportunity to get free for a layup. But a funny thing happened on the way to the execution of the play."

Instead of passing the ball, Lucas simply took the ball to the basket, backing in and ramming home a turn-around jumper that put the Blazers up 101-100 with 11 seconds remaining.

The Nuggets tried to counter by getting the ball to Thompson, but the Blazers overplayed him and forced a desperation shot by Ted McClain that missed as time ran out.

The home-court advantage had been overturned, and the Blazers were jubilant.

"I was elated, hugging Jack McKinney in celebration," Ramsay said. "Even Ron Culp, our unflappable trainer, joined in the cheering. As the din subsided, I called for everyone's attention. Looking sternly in Lucas' direction, I announced in as solemn a voice as I could manage: 'Luke, you're fined $50 for not running the play.' But the joke was too obvious, and I couldn't keep from grinning."

The Blazers now had a throttlehold on the series, and they never released it. Denver got even with a 121-110 victory behind Issel's 36 points in the second game, but then it was on to Portland and some serious home cooking. Not to mention ear-shattering support from the crowd that now had become full-fledged Blazermaniacs.

Those third and fourth games at the Coliseum were tough—Thompson went off for 40 in Game Three—but the Blazers wouldn't crack. They took a 3-1 series lead with 110-106 and 105-96 victories and stood just one game away from a Western Conference showdown with the mighty Lakers.

Denver prolonged the suspense with a 114-105 overtime victory in the fifth game, but even in defeat the Blazers offered up a preview of what was soon to come. They outscored Denver 28-14 in the fourth quarter and thus were able to force overtime.

There was a bit of apprehension surrounding Game Six back in Portland. For one thing, Twardzik had sprained his ankle in the previous game. And just to make matters a little dicier, TV scheduling had forced a situation where the teams had to fly to Oregon and come right back on the court the following day. The Blazers were understandably wary of back-to-back assignments, because there was always concern about Walton's ankles and he desperately needed some rest.

It was no help to the Nuggets, however, as the Blazers delighted their roaring loyalists by zooming off to a 33-16 lead and never looking back. Ramsay had been telling Davis, his prized rookie, that sooner or later he

would be needed in a crucial situation, and this was it. Johnny responded to his first playoff starting role with 25 points on 10-of-14 shooting from the floor. Hollins added 21 points of his own as the Blazers closed ranks to make up for Twardzik's absence.

And so it came down to a matchup with the Lakers—Walton facing majestic Kareem Abdul-Jabbar, the all-world player who preceded him in those dynasty days at UCLA. "Going against Kareem with everything at stake was always my dream," Walton said. "It was the kind of thing that never left my mind. Me and Kareem. Man on man. It was exactly what I'd always wanted."

The Lakers had plenty of reason to be confident going into the series—after all, they'd won three of four regular-season games from Portland—but their swagger

disappeared almost immediately. While a stunned crowd looked on at the Forum in Los Angeles, the Blazers opened up with one of their best games of the year. They employed a plan Ramsay and McKinney had devised to deprive Jabbar of the ball in his favorite spot, simply by forcing the Lakers guards to bring the ball up on the wrong side of the floor to properly start their offense.

Clicking on all cylinders, the Blazers raced off to a 61-43 halftime lead and galloped in from there for a 121-109 victory that rocked the Lakers right down to their sneakers. Not only had the glamour boys from L.A. lost their homecourt edge, they'd clearly been

It fell on Portland's Bobby Gross to try to contain Dr. J. This three-frame sequence by photographer Roger Jensen portrays the challenge Gross faced.

dominated in every phase of the game as Lucas, Hollins, Walton and Davis all scored 20 or more points. The Lakers' psyches had been seriously damaged, and any mental advantage they might have had was erased.

Game Two at the Forum was a different matter altogether. And this one came down, ultimately, to a decision made earlier in the season by one of the Blazers' reserves. Gilliam occasionally had talked about his lack of playing time in the deep Portland backcourt, and Glickman offered the veteran guard the opportunity to leave. A deal with New Orleans was pending, a trade which would have given Gilliam the chance to

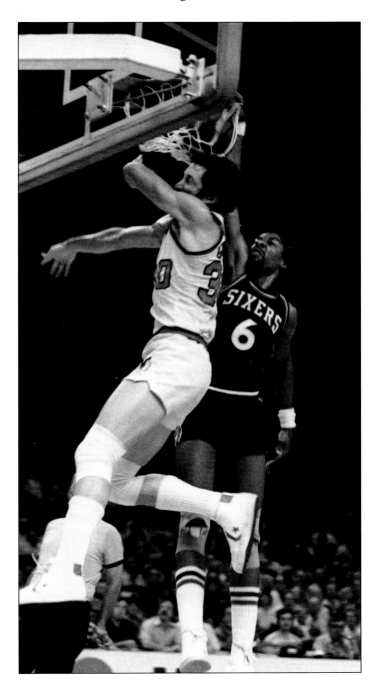

be a starter. And the call was his.

After talking over the situation with his wife and mulling the option of being a role player on a potential champion versus more minutes for a team going nowhere, Gilliam elected to stay with the Blazers. And in the second game of the Lakers series, that choice proved almost divinely inspired.

Los Angeles turned up the defensive heat this time around, wiped out a 54-51 halftime deficit and led 77-70 heading into the fourth quarter. At which point Gilliam went wild, scoring 14 of his 24 points on a variety of seemingly impossible shots. Gilliam wound up 12 of 18 from the floor as the Blazers won 99-97.

Years later, that victory in Los Angeles is remembered simply as "Herm's Game"—even though Hollins scored 31 points to go with seven assists and eight steals.

"I told Bill and Lloyd (Neal) at the half that I thought I ought to be shooting more," Gilliam said. "They were packing in a lot in the middle and we knew we had to shoot more from outside. I've always been more of a one-on-one player but I'm a team man now. But I had to take some of those one-on-one shots in the fourth quarter. They're not the kind of shots Jack wants me to take but they went in."

Ramsay wasn't complaining.

"We call Gilliam 'The Trickster,' "the coach said, "and he threw in some trick shots today. To win these types of games, you have to have somebody do these special things."

Suddenly and improbably up two-zip, the Blazers returned home to find a delirious, howling crowd of several thousand waiting at the airport. Portland was simply in a frenzy. Cries of "Sweep!" were in the air, and although Ramsay and Co. took the party line and predicted rugged battles at the Coliseum from the cornered Lakers, this time the fans were calling it right.

The Blazers did complete their whitewash job on Los Angeles as Walton battled Jabbar tooth and nail, forcing the Lakers supporting cast to pick up the slack—and as Ramsay had suspected and hoped, his deep and relentless club had far more complementary weapons. Portland won the third game 102-97 as Walton scored 14 of his 22 points in the fourth quarter, then closed out the Lakers 105-101 in a furious struggle that proved both the Blazers' resourcefulness and the Lakers' heart.

"They're too proud to just go away, even down three-nothing," Ramsay said. "I told our guys to be ready for the full treatment, and that's what we got."

Once again it was Davis who was in the middle of

The Blazers' speed, precision passing and execution exacted a heavy toll on the talented Sixers.

things down the stretch. He bolted downcourt to score and give Portland a 98-91 lead with 3:36 left, then converted a steal off Jabbar to make it 103-93 and essentially seal the deal. All that speed from Davis, Hollins and Co. had been critical throughout the series.

"We couldn't give Kareem enough help," Lakers coach Jerry West said after the final defeat. "Portland was too quick. They went by us at times like a shoemaker had nailed us to the floor."

As for the titanic duel between Walton and Abdul-Jabbar, it actually made each man look all that much greater. Walton was fantastic—keying the offense, grabbing key rebounds, rejecting shots and, most important, using guile and muscle to force Kareem away from his favorite sky-hook spots. But Jabbar, who averaged 30 points and 16 rebounds despite carrying almost a one-man load, was equally heroic.

Walton did have one majestic moment all to himself, when he threw down a thunderous dunk directly over Jabbar in Game Three. That one had the Blazers bench rocking, and even Kareem responded a day later.

"I know Bill is enjoying this," he said. "It's not Amsterdam Avenue back on the playgrounds, but if he jams a couple, I've got to get the baskets back, so I dunk. I like the way the Blazers play. They should be national champs."

Prophetic words, as it turned out. Soon enough, the Blazers would make Jabbar's prediction a reality. All it took was an astonishing turnaround from a 0-2 deficit against the most talented team in the universe. The 76ers found out for themselves in the Finals what so many victims already had discovered: The Blazers had Walton, and every other answer, too.

Of course, the deciding series didn't exactly start out the way the Blazers would have drawn it up. Because they'd swept the Lakers—and also because of more juggling for television—the Blazers sat idle for a week prior to opening in Philadelphia. It showed, too, as the Sixers parlayed 34 Portland turnovers into a 107-101 victory.

There was some speculation after Game One that perhaps the fabulous Erving was unstoppable. He'd scored 33 points on a variety of acrobatic moves, but Gross—the man primarily responsible for coverage—refused to concede that the task was hopeless. "He's a great player, but everything he does can be stopped," Gross said. "I think I overplayed him too much. It would be better for me to play him straight and just work harder to be in the right spot."

The second game wasn't about defensive positioning,

Bobby Gross was THE MAN in Portland's breakthrough Game Five win in Philadelphia. Gross scored 25 points on 10-of-13 shooting and added five rebounds and five steals.

Portland's camaraderie made for happy times.

however. This one developed more like a heavyweight title fight, with the signature moment a fracas that developed between Lucas and Philadelphia's 6-foot-11, 265-pound man-child, Darryl Dawkins. Late in the 76ers' 107-89 victory, tension that had been building all evening finally boiled over. The two bruisers squared off, with a frantic Ramsay leaping into the middle as peacemaker despite officials' warnings to stay away.

Ironically, the only damage done was to Collins, who was also trying to calm things down. Instead, he caught a wild Dawkins swing over his right eye. It was suggested much later that Collins' blindsiding by a teammate's haymaker actually helped turn around the entire Finals.

Two things were clear, though, by the time the teams left Philly for Oregon. The Sixers believed they had a chokehold on the championship and panic was setting in back in Portland. Newspaper headlines cried out over the Blazers' inexperience finally being exposed, about whether the team was tough enough to win, about how the 76ers might just be too good.

Right after McGinnis slammed down a two-handed monster dunk during Philly's last big run in Game

Two, the Spectrum scoreboard flashed this message: "The Greatest Show on Earth Salutes the Greatest Team on Earth." The reference was to a circus that would be occupying the building while the series moved to Portland, but the point was perfectly clear.

Ramsay wasn't buying any of it. In his post-game remarks to the team and later on the trip home, he told players, staff and the media that no way—absolutely no way—was this series over and that the Blazers needed only to find their normal stride to get back in it. Ramsay, who had been taunted and harassed by Philadelphia fans as he left the Spectrum, was more concerned about a possible lineup change: He considered returning the now-healthy Twardzik to his starting group to restore some poise, then rejected the idea lest he convey the notion that he'd lost faith.

It worked out. Game Three opened with Lucas trot-

Coach Jack Ramsay kept the Blazers focused, even after Philadelphia jumped to a 2-0 series lead.

Twardzik's tenacious style made him invaluable.

ting over to shake hands with Dawkins as the lineups were introduced, and then the Blazers proceeded to lay some serious lumber on the "unbeatable" 76ers. Portland ran at will for a 129-107 win in the third game and followed that with a 130-98 pasting to deadlock the series. Walton summed up the two-game reversal quite simply: "We just went back to playing our game. That's the way we usually play."

Even the 76ers were impressed. "It was like a clinic," Collins said. "I don't see how they could play any better," McGinnis added. "They just took it to us and never let up."

Suddenly, there was serious question about which team deserved that tag of "Greatest Team on Earth."

One thing had become clear: The Blazers hadn't lost a single playoff game at home and didn't appear to be likely candidates for it, so Game Five back in Philly loomed huge. The 76ers desperately needed to restore order, protect the home-court advantage and convince themselves that they weren't going to be run right out of town.

They darn near were. The Blazers produced a 40-point quarter to stun the Spectrum audience, building an 85-64 lead and making it look easy. As they'd done to the Lakers, the Blazers simply beat the Sixers up and

down the floor with withering defense and crisp passing off their fast break.

Philadelphia fought back, but in vain as the Blazers scored their breakthrough 110-104 triumph. "We came back (within six points), but we never had a chance to win," said embattled Sixers coach Gene Shue. "Portland had the game under control completely after we let them dominate us in the third quarter."

In a bit of poetic justice, it was Gross—the guy under fire trying to stop Dr. J—who went crazy in the pivotal fifth game. Gross scored 25 points on 10-of-13 shooting and added five assists and five steals.

"Bobby just broke loose and went on some kind of spree," said Lucas, who had 20 points and 13 rebounds of his own. "He gave us the lift just when we needed it."

And so the stage was set for that now-famous Game Six and the day Oregon will never forget. Beautiful basketball on both sides—at last—and for Portland at least, a beautiful result. All the frustrations of being basically ignored by the rest of the nation erupted when McGinnis missed his historic shot and the Blazers became champions of all they surveyed.

"It's like the roof just blew off the Coliseum in one instant," owner Weinberg recalled of the triumphant moment. "I'm sure I'll never see anything like it again."

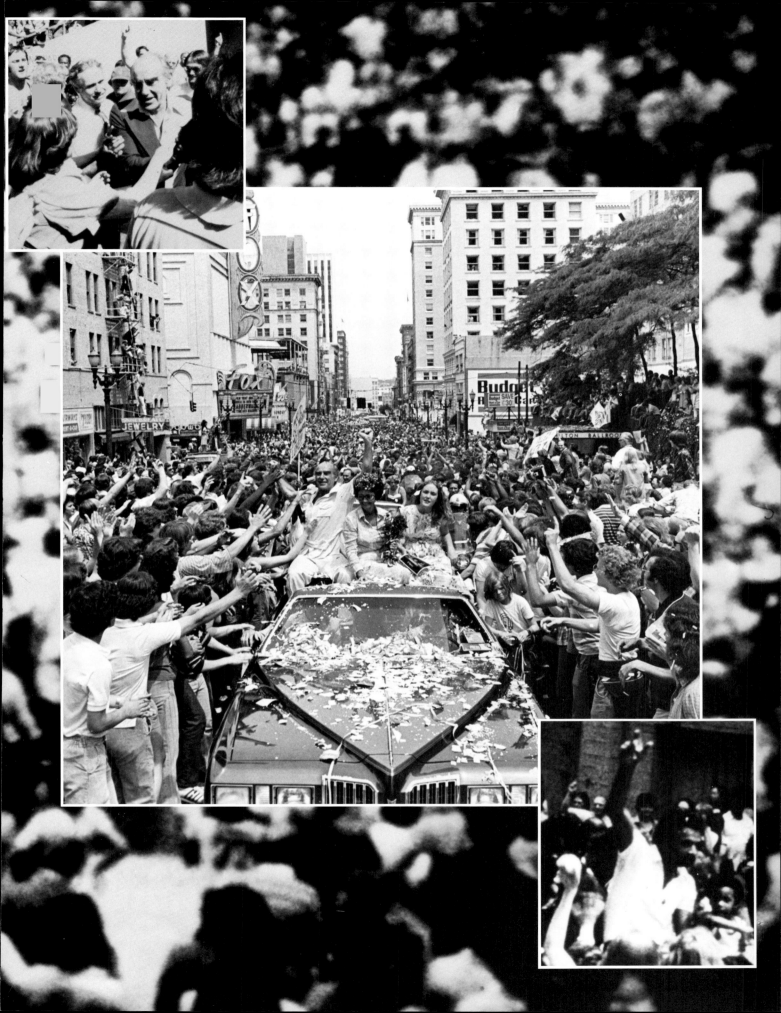

Who will?

Blazers fans remember as though it were yesterday the exhilaration of watching Walton rip off his uniform jersey and hurl it into the crowd just a heartbeat after the final buzzer. Oregonians of that era all claim they were there—or at least at the Monday parade and celebration in Terry Schrunk Plaza. The funny thing is that most of 'em probably were in that giddy mob scene, since crowd estimates ran up past a quarter-million.

"I'll never be able to think of that Monday without smiling," Glickman said. "It was just such a great day for Portland and the whole state. That was Blazermania. Everybody had signs that said, 'Rip City,' or 'Red-Hot and Rollin'—or whatever else they could scribble down."

Walton and his wife, Susan, came to the victory parade on bicycles, never dreaming how many people would jam downtown Portland. They finally had to jump in a car, leading to an amusing postscript when Walton's bike was returned to him by someone who asked only to meet him as a reward.

"It was a love affair between a team and a community and a state," Weinberg said. "It was so special, it's still very hard to describe."

Glickman saved his best line of the season for the celebration podium. Remembering that many in the Philly traveling party had groused about the Portland weather during the Sixers' visits, Glickman told the roaring crowd: "I have a scoop for the Philadelphia media—it ain't raining on our parade today."

Even years later, it seems that Spring of 1977 was nothing but sunshine in Portland.

CHAPTER 3

The NBA Comes to Coos Bay

"*T*HEY WEREN'T VERY GOOD THE FIRST FEW YEARS, BUT THEY SURE WERE A LOT OF FUN."

—BILL SCHONELY

BY NOW, JUST ABOUT EVERYONE'S HEARD THE STORY OF HARRY GLICKMAN'S RAINCOAT.

THE BLAZERS' GODFATHER AND NOW PRESIDENT EMERITUS SPUN THE YARN AGAIN IN HIS FOREWORD TO THIS BOOK, BUT IT DOESN'T LOSE A THING IN REPETITION. THE POINT IS: PORTLAND ALMOST MISSED LANDING THE TRAIL BLAZERS IN THE EXPANSION OF 1970, AND NO MATTER WHAT ELSE MIGHT HAVE HAPPENED DOWN THE ROAD, THAT WOULD HAVE BEEN A SHAME.

You see, the Blazers have been lucky. Not just fortunate that Glickman forgot his raincoat in a Los Angeles hotel room and thus had to return—thereby catching a phone call from the investors who ultimately brought Portland into pro basketball. No, the Blazers and their fans have had an angel on their shoulders every step of the way.

Consider a litany of things that might have gone wrong, that could have tossed Portland into the same sports barrel as so many other cities. Yet every pothole somehow was avoided, and here you find a thriving franchise that has won tons of friends and ballgames and, more important, maintained its place

Harry Glickman's tireless phone calls were a big part of the Blazers success.

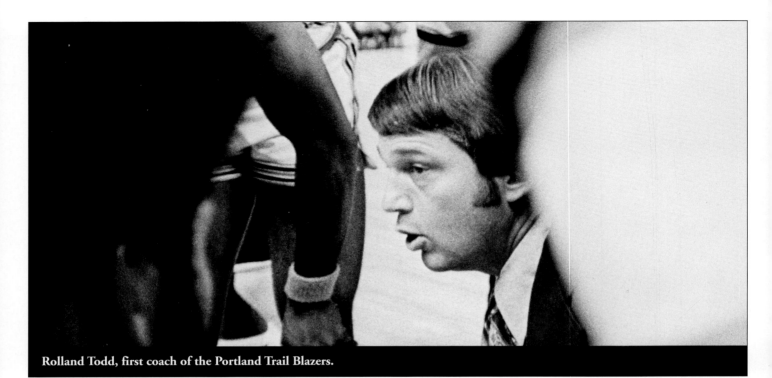

Rolland Todd, first coach of the Portland Trail Blazers.

as a solid corporate citizen. Thank the ownership.

Just for fun, take a peek around the sports world and check out which franchises work and which ones struggle. Almost without exception, you find the winners where there's stability among the folks who put up the bucks. Portland has had three owners — bosses who were footing the bills and calling shots—and each has been the perfect man for his tenure with the club. Even more remarkable is that none of the three—Herman Sarkowsky, Larry Weinberg or Paul Allen— ever has lived in Portland, yet all of them have run the Blazers with the best interests of the community at heart. That's not just rare in the sports biz, it's almost miraculous.

Still think the Blazers' stroll to a place in the NBA sunshine was all just a walk in the park?

It was a phone call from Herman Sarkowsky, right, to Harry Glickman in a Los Angeles hotel room that turned the tide in favor of Portland's bid for an NBA franchise in 1970.

Sure, things seem so wonderful now, with a quarter-century of success in the bank and a glistening new arena under construction, but it didn't have to work out that way. There were no guarantees. "Sometimes I feel blessed," Glickman said, "because every time we got a bad break, something happened to turn things around. And every time we needed a good break, we got it. Most people don't remember how close a call it was just getting the franchise in the first place."

Which brings you back to the raincoat.

Glickman already was a respected sports promoter and boss of the Western Hockey League Portland Buckaroos when he began his flirtation with the NBA in 1969. Portland got its first good turn when Glickman—though he was admittedly starry-eyed about pro basket-ball—turned down an

NBA Commissioner Walter Kennedy, left, Harry Glickman, and Oregon Gov. Tom McCall right are on hand to celebrate the Blazers' first regular season game on Oct. 7, 1970.

NBA Commissioner Walter Kennedy tosses a coin to decide whether Portland or Philadelphia will get the No. 1 pick in the 1974 NBA Draft. On the left are Herman Sarkowsky and Larry Weinberg, Portland's president and treasurer respectively, and on the right is Irv Kosloff, president of the Sixers. Philadelphia called heads and the coin came up tails, giving Portland the right to go after UCLA All-American Bill Walton.

offer to work for Los Angeles Lakers owner Jack Kent Cooke. Glickman decided he'd rather try to fetch a franchise for his hometown.

It wasn't easy. Even though Walter Kennedy, the league's commissioner, was a proponent both of expansion—Chicago, Seattle, San Diego, Milwaukee and Phoenix all had joined the league in the previous four years—and Portland, some league owners wanted to

structure any future deal in such a way that new teams would not share fully in TV revenues, which were expected to increase dramatically.

Glickman and his attorney, Moe Tonkon, attended a meeting in Philadelphia during the NBA's All-Star weekend in 1970. Four cities—Portland, Cleveland, Houston and Buffalo—were applying for franchises, and the rumor was that two of the four would be

Harry Glickman and Lenny Wilkens are enjoying it at a May 24, 1974 press conference at which Wilkens was named the Blazers' fourth head coach.

Making a point, Rolland Todd huddles with his players.

admitted to the league that weekend. Instead, everyone left in a huff when the owners jacked up the asking price from $3 million to $4 million and announced that any new teams would be cut off from television money for three years.

"In all my 45 years of practicing law, I have never been dealt with so shabbily," Tonkon fumed at the NBA owners. "Here you have a committee which has invited our application, the commissioner has told us what the purchase price would be, and now you intend to go back on your word. Under the circumstances, Portland would have no interest in joining."

That could have been the end of it, but Glickman kept an open mind when some members of the league's expansion commit-

Harry Glickman poses with Portland's first Trail Blazer, Geoff Petrie of Princeton.

tee —Seattle's Sam Schulman and Abe Pollin of Baltimore were among the most encouraging—kept in touch and showed some flexibility when Harry suggested a fairer shake. What Glickman ultimately got was a deal that bumped the price to $3.7 million but made new teams full partners in any revenue.

But Portland still didn't have an ownership group. Glickman couldn't exactly ask for a franchise and say he'd find the money later. There weren't any big-bucks takers in town, either. Glickman recalled hearing this advice from Gerry Pratt, financial editor of *The Oregonian*: "Remember, people in Oregon with a lot of money want anonymity, not notoriety."

The best chance seemed to be a public stock offering, but that still left the matter of interim financing. The

NBA wouldn't grant a franchise on the basis of a stock sale that hadn't even taken place. It would be like the league loaning money to a business without a single stockholder. As the February 6 meeting of the expansion committee drew closer, Glickman became pessimistic that anyone would step forward with enough money to land a team.

That's how Sarkowsky, a Seattle developer, got into the picture. And what led to the now-famous phone call. Sarkowsky told Glickman he'd take a significant ownership piece of the franchise if he could persuade a couple of his business acquaintances to join him. So Glickman left for Los Angeles wondering if he'd ever hear back from anyone.

Sarkowsky's friends turned out to be Weinberg and Bob Schmertz, two other men who had been successful

68

in the home-building business in different parts of the country—Weinberg in southern California and Schmertz in New Jersey.

"Herm and I had been close friends for a long time," Weinberg said. "We'd been involved in forming a group called the Master Homebuilders Conference, which met two or three times a year. Around 1970, it was suggested that we all get into a project together. The idea was it would be something enjoyable, something outside our usual business. And it came up that ownership of a sports franchise was a possibility.

"I remember saying that I was only interested if the

Again, providence seemed to be working in Portland's favor.

So it came down to that fateful expansion meeting, at which Glickman felt sure he was departing disappointed because no one had stepped forward with any money. But as most Blazers fans recall so happily, Harry left his raincoat in Pollin's hotel suite, where the meeting had been held. When he went back to retrieve the coat, there was a call from Sarkowsky. A last-second savior had ridden to the rescue.

Yes! The ownership group was intact, and Portland was headed into the NBA.

Stu Inman, the Blazer's first director of player personnel and general manager, gestures to coach Jack Ramsay as they prepare for the NBA's '82 draft. Assistant coach Jimmy Lynam listens in. The Blazers made Arizona State guard Lafayette Lever their first pick.

sport was basketball. So we looked around to see where we could buy a franchise. I lived in Los Angeles and knew there was a team floundering in San Diego, so I inquired about that, but no one even returned my phone call. It was at that point that Herm called about the expansion possibility in Portland. I'd only been in Portland once or twice in my life, but I liked it. Ironically, one of the times I'd been up there, I went to see a pro football exhibition game put on by Harry Glickman."

So Glickman's raincoat became a part of Trail Blazers lore, which begs an intriguing question. Why in the world had Harry lugged the garment to sunny Los Angeles in the first place? "I guess it was habit," he said. "When you live in Portland and you're going someplace in February, you're going to be carrying a raincoat. But I don't really even remember taking it to the meeting. You just get used to carrying a raincoat, I suppose."

Whenever Blazers fans are moved to curse those dark, gloomy clouds that often seem to swallow up Portland,

Coach Lenny Wilkens gives instruction to former Oregon and ABA star guard Steve Jones. Jones played one season for the Blazers before becoming a standout broadcast analyst and sports call-in host for the organization.

Three of the four men who came together to launch the Portland franchise in 1970. From left, Harry Glickman, the team's founder; Herman Sarkowsky, the first president of the Blazers; and Larry Weinberg, treasurer the first year, and later president. It was the capital put up by Sarkowsky, Weinberg and Robert Schmertz, that assured Portland of being granted an expansion team. The picture was taken at a 1992 banquet honoring Glickman as Portland's First Citizen.

Jack McCloskey, left, and his assistant, Neil Johnston,
at the start of the 1972-73 season. Johnston, a future inductee
in the Basketball Hall of Fame, was Portland's first assistant coach.

Geoff Petrie drives against future Hall of Famer Jerry West.

Rick Adelman

Shaler Halimon

Jim Barnett

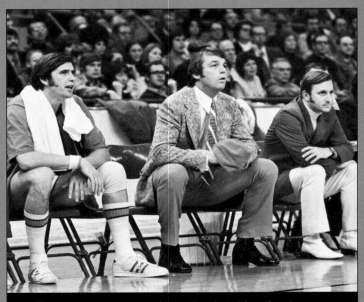

Geoff Petrie sits next to coach Rolland Todd and trainer Leo Marty *(left to right).* Todd and Marty made up the entire staff that first year.

Walt Gilmore

Gary Gregor

Ed Manning

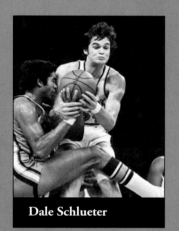

Dale Schlueter

Ron Knight

LeRoy Ellis

Claude English

Stan McKenzie

they at least can smile and realize that the town's regular dose of rain most likely was responsible for Glickman toting the coat that brought them a basketball team.

However close a call it had been, the Blazers were born and scheduled to begin play in the 1970-71 season. Weinberg remembered it as one of the most delightful times in franchise history. "However, I did have one jarring conversation before we even got started," he said. "I met with Dick Bloch, the Phoenix Suns owner, at the Brown Derby restaurant in L.A. Here we were all excited about joining the NBA and Dick said, 'You guys are idiots. You paid too much, and your team

in North Carolina. He had charisma, and when he got cut, he was devastated, and so were my kids. We all wondered: What's he going to do now? It was all part of the naive sort of enjoyment we got from the first days of the Blazers.

"No one expected a championship in our first, second or even third years. But we all agreed we wanted to build a team with the characteristics of playing hard, scrapping for every ball, fighting to win every game. That was going to be the Trail Blazers' trademark: From Day One, we would be a team that never gave up, that never threw in the chips. We were determined on that,

Lenny Wilkens sits alongside his assistant, Tom Meschery.

isn't even going to get the ball until after we score.' How's that for a welcome into the league?

"Still, the early days were really fun for everyone. Naturally, we knew that we wouldn't be winning any championships right away, but that was OK. Everyone got really attached to some of the players who came and went in the first few years. I remember taking my kids up to rookie camp. We learned about the players and how tough it really was to make it in the NBA. The kids got attached to certain players and rooted for them. One guy that sticks in my mind was a kid named Israel Oliver, from Elizabeth City State, a little school

and also that we would do everything in our power to build through scouting—with guys like Stu (Inman) and later on Bucky (Buckwalter)—and that we'd never close our minds to new or unconventional ideas. Those were Blazers characteristics from the beginning and, really, they've never changed, which is one reason the team has been so successful for so many years."

Glickman made a few decisions right at the beginning which shaped the franchise, too.

First off, he needed a player personnel guru, and hired Inman after just one intense meeting at the Portland airport. Inman was anointed on the spot and flew off to

Lenny Wilkens became player-coach of the Trail Blazers in 1974 after filling similar roles at Seattle and Cleveland. Now a member of the Basketball Hall of Fame, Wilkens played in his last game in Portland on April 6, 1975, scoring 15 points in a 126-97 win over the Los Angeles Lakers.

his first college scouting assignment without ever leaving the airport.

Then there was the matter of a radio announcer, somebody who would be the first voice of the Blazers. This is a terribly important call for an expansion team, because the radio guy also becomes your chief salesman, hopefully transmitting excitement to a brand-new audience unfamiliar with the league. In Portland, the decision was especially critical

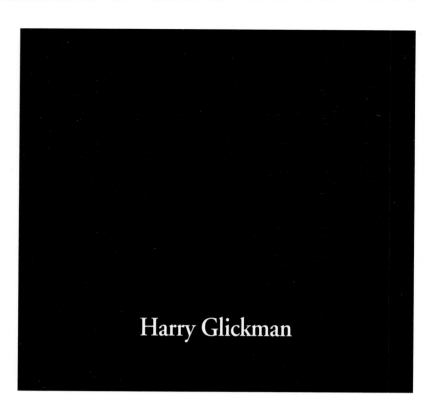

Harry Glickman

because, while the good citizens of Oregon did have considerable knowledge of college basketball, they were neophytes to the pro game. And they'd never been involved with a major-league professional team in any sport.

It's pretty obvious Glickman struck gold on this one, landing Bill Schonely, whom he'd known from a stint with Seattle in the Western Hockey League. Not only did The Schonz do a bang-up job pitching

Bill Walton, who suffered a fractured foot 35 games into his rookie season, watches from the bench beside assistant coach Tom Meschery and player-coach Lenny Wilkens.

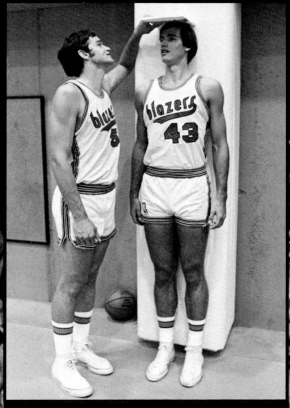

Bill Smith (No. 43) was Portland's first seven foot tall center. Veteran post player Dale Schleuter, who stands 6-foot-10, verifies the seven foot measurement.

Jack McCloskey

Future NBA coaches Rick Adelman and Lenny Wilkens had many memorable battles on the court. Here they go against each other when Lenny was player-coach with Seattle.

Bill Smith, drafted in the third round out of Syracuse in 1971, showed real promise at center until a broken leg late in his rookie season brought an end to his basketball career.

the NBA, he stuck around to become a true Blazers legend.

"Over the years, Schonz has gone way beyond being just an announcer," said current Blazers communications director John Lashway. "He kind of became the team itself. Schonz is probably a bigger name in Oregon than any one individual player. It's really pretty incredible. He's a phenomenon. I honestly don't think it could have happened with any other guy or in any other market. Everybody identifies with Schonz."

Funny how things work out. Glickman can laugh about it now, but Schonely wasn't his first choice for the radio job. Glickman always had admired the work of another former Seattle broadcaster, Les Keiter. Schonz got the call because Keiter was committed to taking another job.

One other critical decision, though, was all Glickman's and looking back, it was a stroke of genius. Harry decided from the outset that in the Blazers' smallish market, he needed to involve the entire state of Oregon.

Jack McCloskey erupts after his Blazers score at the other end of the floor.

"You look around now and see every town in the state caught up in the Blazers, and that was all Harry's doing," said Geoff Petrie, who was the team's first-ever No. 1 draft choice and much later presided over those championship runs of 1990 and '92 as the club's general manager. "From the very beginning, we were packed off on buses to play exhibition games all over Oregon. Some of those little high school gyms really couldn't

handle it, but somehow that just added to the excitement. It was an unbelievable event when the Blazers came to town. Think about it: Pro basketball in Coos Bay?

"Remember, we weren't exactly household names, not even in Portland at the beginning. I've told the story at a lot of banquets about going into a bank to deposit a check and having the clerk ask me who the Portland Trail Blazers were. But Harry made up his mind that we—players, staff, everybody—would get out into the community and that we'd be visible all over the state. That decision definitely sowed the seeds for the popularity the Blazers enjoy now."

It's easy these days to see the incredible string of sellouts the Blazers have enjoyed at Memorial Coliseum and assume the mania existed right from the start, but that's not how it happened.

Rick Adelman, the Blazers' first captain and later their highly successful coach, recalled the never-ending battle to lure fans to this NBA venture. "We only had five or six people in the front office back then," Adelman said. "It was so different. I had a job selling season tickets in the off-season. Remember, Harry still owned the Buckaroos at that time and their goalie, Jimmy McLeod, had the same job I did."

Was Adelman good at it?

"I didn't do as well as I hoped," he said with a chuckle. "I think it was because the secretary in our office

Leo Marty, Portland's first trainer, issues uniforms to Sidney Wicks and Charles Yelverton, the Blazers' first two draft picks in 1971.

PRESIDENT GERALD FORD sat behind the Portland bench in Memorial Coliseum on November 1, 1974, to watch the Trail Blazers and the Buffalo Braves go at it in a regular season game. According to sources in the White House, it was the first time a U.S. president had attended a National Basketball Association game. To President Ford's right is U.S. Sen. Bob Packwood (R-Ore.), and to his left is Oregon Gov. Tom McCall. In the foreground, from left, Blazers trainer Ron Culp, security guard John Schaeffer, and assistant coach Tom Meschery.

loved hockey and she was giving McLeod all the best leads."

There were still plenty of empty seats most nights in those first few seasons. "I can testify to that," Adelman said. "There was one guy who used to get on me at every game. As far as this guy was concerned, I couldn't do anything right, and he hollered at me non-stop. If it had been a few years later, with the building full and everybody screaming, you wouldn't notice. But with some small crowds, one person with a loud voice could be heard, believe me. I can still hear him."

Consistent with the philosophy that they wanted a thrill-a-minute team right from the outset, the Blazers brass selected UNLV's Rolland Todd as their first coach because, among other things, he was a proponent of hurry-up, fast-tempo basketball. And right on cue, Todd's maiden team in 1970-71 startled everyone by winning 29 games and playing well against several established clubs—especially at home.

Sure, the schedule was weighted so that the three expansion teams that season played each other a disproportionate number of times, but wins are wins.

"We finished with a better record than the other two expansion teams and we upset some big-name teams at the Coliseum," said Petrie, who came out of Princeton to play all 82 games and average 24.8 points. Petrie wound up sharing NBA Rookie of the Year honors with Boston's Dave Cowens, so his draft selection was nothing less than a coup.

That first team, which put together a couple of five-game winning streaks, also got great years from Jim Barnett, a local hero from the University of Oregon who was obtained in a preseason trade with San Diego for Larry Siegfried. And then the Blazers did some wheeling and dealing with other teams in order to grab center LeRoy Ellis in the expansion draft. Both moves paid off as Barnett (18.4 points per game) and Ellis (15.9) each had good seasons for the first-year Blazers.

Glickman, Inman and Co. had no illusions that they could build the future around such clever trading, however. They had much different long-term plans.

"The organizations I most admired in professional sports were the Minnesota Vikings and Dallas Cowboys in the National Football League and the Montreal

Schlueter goes
one-on-one with the
huge Wilt Chamberlain.

Lloyd Neal goes up against the Bulls' Artis Gilmore.

dering and then was put together via the draft was the champion New York Knicks of 1970 and '73. Their mainstays—Willis Reed, Walt Frazier and Bill Bradley were draft choices. Once they had put this lineup together, Eddie Donovan, their general manager, found himself in the fortunate position of being able to make a trade for Dave DeBusschere. That cemented their lineup and enabled them to win two NBA championships."

Thus the Blazers were committed from the beginning to building from the ground up. And history has proven Glickman correct. Portland's best teams through the years have been anchored by draft picks—Bill Walton, Bobby Gross, Lionel Hollins, Johnny Davis, Lloyd Neal, Larry Steele and Dave Twardzik from the title gang of 1977 to Clyde Drexler, Jerome Kersey, Terry Porter and Clifford Robinson on the great clubs of the early 1990s. On the other hand, when the Blazers tried

Sidney Wicks is hounded by Phoenix's Paul Silas.

Canadiens in the National Hockey League," Glickman said. "The Vikings and Cowboys were both expansion teams who had played in Portland during their first year of operation. They were terrible but they were built steadily and patiently. Once they achieved success, they were able to remain contenders over a long period of years. This was the formula I wanted to use for the Trail Blazers.

"It's not that I consider trades unimportant, but there has never been a genius in our business who has traded his way to a championship. Colleges offer us the greatest farm system ever devised. We not only obtain highly skilled and talented basketball players every year, but we also obtain instant attractions at the gate.

"One of the best examples of a team that was floun-

When 6-7 Lloyd Neal stepped in at the center spot for
Portland, he too faced a height deficit as demonstrated
in his matchup with Abdul-Jabbar

Larry Steele, here against Pete Maravich of Atlanta, was Portland's first ever national statistical leader, topping the NBA in steals in 1974 with an average of 2.7 per game.

Background: Sidney Wicks could score points and rebound but he also feuded with his teammates, including Geoff Petrie.

Sidney Wicks, working here against Houston's Rudy Tomjanovich, won Rookie of the Year honors in 1972, the second consecutive Portland player to be so recognized.

the opposite approach —restructuring the entire team with a trade for Denver's Kiki Vandeweghe prior to the 1984-85 season—they went just 82-82 over the next

Blazers president Herman Sarkowsky presents the 1971 NBA Rookie of the Year trophy to Geoff Petrie at the first game of the 1971-72 season. Petrie, who shared the honor with Boston's Dave Cowens, remains one of only eight players in the history of the NBA to tally 2,000 or more points in their rookie year. The others: Walt Bellamy, Rick Barry, Wilt Chamberlain, Oscar Robertson, Elvin Hayes, Kareem Abdul-Jabbar, and most recently, Michael Jordan.

couple of years and Hall of Fame coach Jack Ramsay lost his job.

Predictably, the Blazers weren't very good in those first few build-up seasons. Todd was fired toward the end of an 18-64 disaster in 1971-72, in part because No. 1 draft choice Sidney Wicks scored a lot of points but turned out to be something less than an ideal team player. Wicks feuded with Petrie and, at one point, criticized the coaches and his teammates in a radio interview. Among other things, Wicks announced: "We stink." It took awhile for the Blazers to dispose of Wicks, but when they did it prior to the 1976-77 season, it helped win a championship.

Jack McCloskey coached the next two years following Todd's dismissal and Lenny Wilkens a couple after that as the Blazers got better (21 wins, then 27, 38 and 37) but not good enough to reach the playoffs. A foundation was being laid, however, and fan interest reflected it. The Blazers averaged 6,135 their first season in the NBA and had only one dip after that (from 8,134 their third year to 7,988 in their fourth, 1973-74) en route to the really big crowds that came to symbolize Portland basketball. Attendance jumped to 10,768 in 1974-75 and once Blazermania truly took hold with the championship season, well, tickets became a precious commodity in Oregon.

It's not that the early years were without their moments, either: The Blazers won their first NBA game, a 115-112 victory over Cleveland on Oct. 16, 1970. The Coliseum was rocking later that season when 10,259 came out for a game with those same Knicks that Glickman admired. Portland lost that game, but then came back and upset the Knicks, 114-96, before 11,868 converts to the thrills of pro basketball.

And here's a trivia note from the first season: Did you know that the Blazers selected Pat Riley in the expan-

Harry Glickman

Geoff Petrie has trouble fighting through this screen set by the Lakers' Wilt Chamberlain for Jerry West.

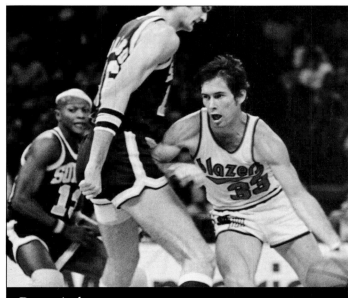

Danny Anderson

A pure scorer: Terry Dischinger

John Johnson

sion draft? He was sold to the Lakers, though, without ever playing a regular-season game for Portland.

Throughout the Blazers' first six seasons, Petrie was magnificent. He remains just the second rookie guard in NBA history—along with the great Oscar Robertson—to score more than 2,000 points. In 1973, Petrie twice scored 51 points in a game, still the franchise's single-game scoring record.

Talk about excitement: Short of the playoffs, it would be hard to top the 1974 home opener, which not only was Walton's debut at the Coliseum but turned into an excruciating marathon as the Blazers outlasted Cleveland 131-129 in four overtimes.

One of the biggest disappointments of the so-called expansion seasons came with the 1972 draft. The Blazers won a coin flip with Buffalo and had the first pick in the whole thing, but contract negotiations with projected choice Bob McAdoo of North Carolina fell apart with plenty of acrimony. Glickman and the Blazers felt that McAdoo and his agent dealt in bad faith; in fact, that they had shaken hands on an agreement and then changed their minds—adding huge demands—the following morning. When Glickman reported that unpleasant news to Sarkowsky, the team president replied: "Tell them to go to hell."

Ollie Johnson

Darrall Imhoff

Unfortunately, the '72 draft was pitifully thin, and the Blazers had almost nowhere to turn after the blowout with McAdoo. Their No. 1 choice turned out to be 6-foot-11 LaRue Martin of Chicago Loyola, who sadly never became the player management thought he would be. That pick was thrown back at the Blazers for years, but actually, 1972 wasn't a total loss. Portland had five choices in the first three rounds of that draft and they weren't all wasted. The Blazers selected Twardzik, for one, and even though he went off to play in the ABA, they retained the rights which brought him back in 1976. And then there was Neal, a sturdy center-forward from Tennessee State who fell to Portland at the 31st overall pick. Neal not only beat out Martin for the starting center position and finished second to McAdoo

Geoff Petrie goes high for
a reverse lay-in
against the Warriors.
Geoff was one of several
Blazers to sport beards
in the mid-1970s.

Wicks and Petrie in rebounding position.

LaRue Martin, the No. 1 pick in the 1972 NBA draft.

for Rookie of the Year, he was still around to provide quality backup punch for the '77 championship team.

Most of all, those early seasons created expectations. Once the gifted but fragile Walton came aboard in 1974, excited fans believed the Blazers were due to leap from scrappy but overmatched novelties to legitimate contenders.

"It was frustrating to take a couple of steps forward and then have something happen or make a mistake which pushed us a step back," Glickman said. "Still, you could feel we were on the right track. The fans kept coming out in bigger numbers, the excitement was growing and it wasn't too long before we were a real NBA team.

"Everybody felt the next big jump would be the play-offs, but who would ever have dreamed that we'd go right on to win a championship the first time we ever had a chance?

"Like every promoter, all I've ever been able to do is plan as well as possible, then open the doors and see what happens. I wish I were smart enough to know it would turn out the way it did with the Blazers.

"Maybe the fans knew more than I did. They kept getting more and more worked up each year. Then all of a sudden, there we were, winning it all. We've always said our fans were knowledgeable, so maybe they knew what was coming all along.

"I just wish they'd told me ahead of time. It would have been easier on my heart."

Geoff Petrie was Portland's first-ever selection to play in the NBA All-Star game. Here he is on the floor with teammates Gail Goodrich (26) and Kareem Abdul-Jabbar (33) against the East's Dave Cowens (18) and Pete Maravich, in the 1974 classic in Seattle.

Lionel Hollins was one of Portland's top floor leaders and averaged 13.6 points in 315 games as a Blazer.

Dave Wohl drives around Oscar Robertson.

Steve Jones

Phil Lumpkin

Terry Dischinger, who played just one season for the Blazers and later became a prominent dentist in the Portland area, here engages in some double-fisted extra curricular activity in a 1973 game against Cleveland. Greg Smith looks on.

Future Kansas City Kings Hall of Famer Tiny Archibald is challenged by Larry Steele.

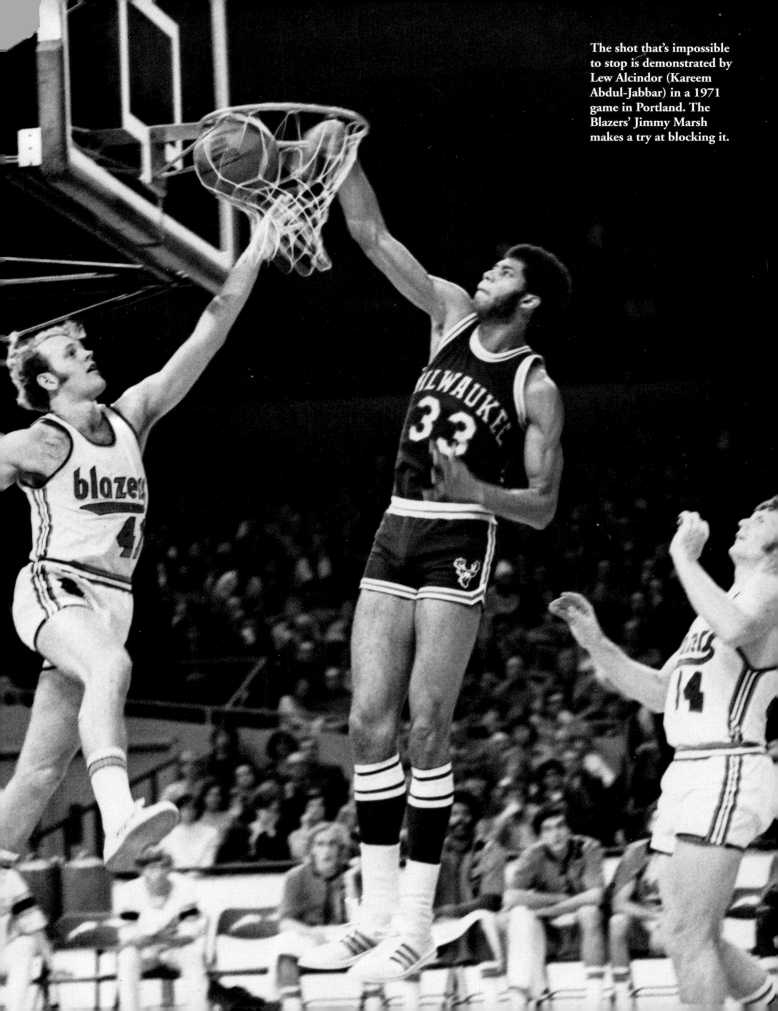

The shot that's impossible to stop is demonstrated by Lew Alcindor (Kareem Abdul-Jabbar) in a 1971 game in Portland. The Blazers' Jimmy Marsh makes a try at blocking it.

At courtside, Petrie & Schonely call a Blazers home game.

Future Golden State Warrior coach Don Nelson (No. 19) as a Boston Celtic battles for a rebound against Terry Dischinger.

Blazers President Larry
Weinberg courtside with
Harley Frankel and a
young Trail Blazers fan.

JAPANESE CONNECTION

The Portland Trail Blazers' opened their 25th Anniversary season 5,500 miles from home, playing the Los Angeles Clippers in a pair of games in Yokohama, Japan. But that wasn't the franchise's first introduction to the blossoming trans-Pacific fascination with the game of basketball. In the summer before Portland's second season, the Trail Blazers rookies and the Japanese National Team shared training camp facilities at Portland's Lewis and Clark College for a week. It was no coincidence that the Japanese team was there to work out, since it was coached by Stu Inman, Blazers' director of player personnel. He shared the coaching task with close friends Pete Newell, ex-University of California head man, and Jack Avina, then the coach at the University of Portland. They were readying their charges for the Asian Games later that summer. The rookies and Japanese players worked out separately but came together for practice scrimmages which drew standing-room only crowds in Pamplin Sports Center. The strong challenge given the visitors by the Blazers' first-year group, headed by the likes of Sidney Wicks and Larry Steele, ultimately paid off. The Japanese team went on to win the Asian Games and qualified for the Olympics in Munich the following summer.

CHAPTER 4

Life After Bill

> "*J*UST THINK ABOUT HOW CLOSE PORTLAND HAS COME TO
> HAVING A REAL DYNASTY—MORE THAN ONCE."
>
> —CLYDE DREXLER

FORGIVE BLAZERS FANS IF THEY SOMETIMES WONDER WHAT MIGHT HAVE BEEN.

YES, THEY REMEMBER THE CHAMPIONSHIP OF 1977 WITH LASTING JOY. THEY SURELY APPRECIATED A DECADE OF PLAY THAT RARELY DIPPED AS LOW AS MEDIOCRE IN THE '80s AND THEY ROARED WITH APPRECIATION WHEN THOSE TAKE-NO-PRISONERS BLAZERS OF THE EARLY 1990s MADE THREE STRAIGHT SERIOUS SHOTS AT ANOTHER TITLE OR TWO.

But it's hard to strike up a basketball conversation in Oregon without at least some reference to a potential dynasty. Several times in the years following the Miracle of '77, Portland seemed on the edge of something truly dramatic— poised perhaps to begin a run reminiscent of, say, the Boston Celtics. Maybe that's a little strong, but a long stretch of years near the top of the NBA—something along the lines of the Lakers, maybe—could have been very much in the cards.

Almost from the moment NBA commissioner Larry O'Brien handed over the championship hardware in '77, the Blazers hurtled headlong into bad, bad luck.

Intense Jerome Kersey claims another rebound.

No, they've never really been down in all the years since, as evidenced by the fact that they've endured only three losing records since Walton and Co. carted home the big trophy, and never had two in a row. They've missed the playoffs just once, won 50-plus games six times under three different coaches — and their worst season since the championship was in 1979-80, when they were 38-44. There are franchises all over the place that ache for such consistency routinely mixed with brilliance.

Still, it's easy for Blazermaniacs to look back occasionally and think: What if...?

Foot injuries, international intrigue worthy of a made-for-TV movie and another of those infernal coin flips all jumped up at various times, preventing the Blazers from leaping toward league domination. For a franchise that has made so many canny moves and played outstanding basketball for close to two decades without interruption, the Blazers honestly can claim

The Blazers traded Sam Bowie to New Jersey for Buck Williams in the summer of 1989.

that they might have been much, much better.

"You can look back at Portland's history and imagine banners flying all over the place at the Coliseum," long-time star Clyde Drexler said. "After I got here (in 1983), we had three different chances to land the type of center who would have made us so good, we would have been scary."

Drexler's math is perfect. He was referring, first of all, to the now-infamous 1984 draft, which featured two blue-chip pivotmen— Hakeem Olajuwon from the University of Houston and Sam Bowie of Kentucky. The Blazers seemed to be in a perfect spot. In 1981, they had traded center Tom Owens to Indiana for the Pacers' first pick in '84, and it turned out to be a coin-flip position for a shot at the No. 1 choice in the entire draft. The NBA abandoned the two-team coin flip for a lottery system the following season.

"You looked at the thing and figured: How could we lose?" said Blazers boss Harry Glickman. "Everybody knew Olajuwon was the best, and

Clyde Drexler drives against his former University of Houston "Phi Slamma Jamma" teammate Hakeem Olajuwon.

sure, we wanted him. But at the time, Bowie looked awfully good, too. He was a shot-blocker, a rebounder and outlet-pass kind of guy who could have fit in perfectly with the type of athletes we were drafting and the full-court game we were determined to play."

Sadly, the Blazers did lose.

They called tails in the coin flip and the doggone

thing came up heads, sending Olajuwon—the league's most recent MVP—to the Houston Rockets. And thus the Blazers chose Bowie, despite knowledge of a foot injury that cost him two full seasons at Kentucky, over a talented shooting guard from North Carolina who went No. 3.

Michael Jordan.

"It's easy now to look back and wish it had gone differently," said Bucky Buckwalter, who has put in 18 years in scouting and player personnel capacities for the Blazers. "We checked all the medical reports on Bowie and believed he was 100 percent. So did everyone else. As for Jordan, well, everybody knew he'd be a good pro player from what they'd seen in college, but no one—I mean, no one—ever guessed that he'd become what he did. Obviously, if you had a crystal ball, Michael would be the No. 1 choice in any draft in history."

And Bowie, unfortunately, broke down. He lasted parts of five seasons in Portland, but was never really healthy. After playing 76 games and averaging 10 points while learning his trade as a rookie in 1984-85, those injury woes returned. Bowie lasted only 38 games the next year, just five the season after that and finally, after treatment, surgery and crossed fingers proved no more use, he was traded along with a No. 1 draft choice to New Jersey in 1989 for Buck Williams. A nice return, but not exactly what the Blazers had in mind back in 1984.

Drexler just shakes his head remembering the entire episode. "To start with, what if we'd won the flip and

Sam Bowie powers one in.

NBA's No. 2 and No. 1 draft choices in 1984—Sam Bowie and Hakeem Olajuwon. The No. 3 selection? Michael Jordan (right) against Clyde Drexler.

gotten Hakeem?" Drexler said of his former college teammate. "Think about Hakeem in the middle with all the guys we've had since then. Oh, man. We'd all have a few rings on our fingers. Sometimes I have dreams about that.

"The other thing is that picking Sam wasn't the wrong move when the organization made it. Yeah, you look at what Michael's done. And Sam got hurt and wasn't ever really the same player. That's just bad luck. But at the time, what we really needed was a center to rebound, get the ball and run—that's our game—and Sam looked like he was perfect for it. People forget just how good Sam Bowie was. He was very good—maybe not like Hakeem, but a heck of a player who would have fit our style. We could have won championships with a healthy Sam Bowie. I believe that."

Remember Drexler's remark about three chances to land a dominant center?

Olajuwon and Bowie were the first two, obviously, but outside Portland, not too many fans recall that just two years after the star-crossed '84 draft, the Blazers took a shot at another spectacular big man. The problem on this occasion was that the Cold War just didn't end soon enough.

The player in question was Arvydas Sabonis, a massive Lithuanian—then just 23 years old but already a star for the Soviet Union's international juggernaut. Sabonis was a gifted giant—7-foot-2, 280 pounds, with an incredible wing

Larry Steele

span and unique skills as both a passer and shooter with remarkable range. "You have to understand that things weren't the same then as they are today," Buckwalter said. "The political climate was completely different. NBA teams weren't going after Eastern European players, or any of the Russians. The thought was that you couldn't get them to America. Everyone figured the good players over there were prisoners of the system, and until 1986, no team in our league ever had used a high draft choice for that type of player. It was considered far too risky for an early-round pick."

The Blazers always had a willingness to be innovative, however, and they decided to take the plunge in '86. Portland used its second selection—24th overall—for a chance to fetch Sabonis out of the Soviet Union. In that same draft, the Blazers chose a Greek frontliner, Panagiotis Fasoulas of North Carolina State, in the second round and Yugoslavian guard Drazen Petrovic in the third.

The selection of Petrovic turned out to be more than just a footnote. He was a gifted outside shooter who did some valuable long-range work for the Blazers as a popular rookie in 1989-90. Petrovic and his agent, however, complained about playing time to Coach Rick Adelman, and Petrovic was traded to New Jersey early the following season. He became a marquee player for the Nets until his tragic death in an automobile accident.

The Blazers' pursuit of Sabonis,

meanwhile, fell just short of full-blown international intrigue. "What happened after that draft was almost unbelievable," Blazers owner Larry Weinberg said. "You could write a book just about our pursuit of Sabonis. Sometimes it felt almost like spy-novel stuff. And it never seemed to end."

There seemed to be no question about Sabonis' potential. "You had to see this guy," Buckwalter said. "Across a room, he looked like just another big man, but then when you got closer, he was really something to look at. He was huge, and not just bulky but really well-built with tremendously long arms. He was a shot-

ed money and we thought we could buy him out. The basketball czars in Lithuania and Russia would have to be paid off, but it looked like it was possible. And Sabonis was young enough that even if it took some time, we felt he would be worth it."

As Weinberg indicated, the saga became storybook stuff. On one occasion, when the Russian team was playing in Spain, Weinberg and Buckwalter used an expatriate go-between to set up a clandestine midnight meeting with Sabonis. The big man let it be known that he had always dreamed of playing in the NBA. He announced that he couldn't simply defect to the United

Drexler lofts a pass to Bowie at the top of the key.

blocker who could pass and shoot—Europeans work a lot on those things—and we felt he could be as good as any big man in the world."

The Blazers also thought that Sabonis might be pried out of the closed Soviet system. The critical point seemed to be that he was Lithuanian—as opposed to an ethnic Russian—and as future events proved out, citizens of the Baltic states were fiercely independent. "We knew we'd have to jump through a lot of hoops," Buckwalter said, "but the federation in Lithuania need-

States because of his family back home, but clearly he was excited at the prospect of making the jump to Portland.

And then Sabonis injured his Achilles tendon prior to the 1988 Olympics.

Another round of negotiations took place—helped along by such diverse individuals as media mogul Ted Turner and industrialist Armand Hammer, both of whom were friendly with the Soviet government. The Blazers offered to bring Sabonis to Portland for treat-

The Trail Blazers'
exhaustive quest
to land massive
Lithuanian center
Arvydas Sabonis
(7-foot-2, 280 pounds)
extended to bringing
the star to Portland
for treatment of a
leg injury in the
summer of 1988.
Portland selected
Sabonis in the
first round of the
1986 NBA draft.

Maurice Lucas takes a jumper in Seattle.

ment on his leg, all the while hoping to find the right people in the Soviet Union to compensate for Sabonis' eventual move into the NBA.

Sabonis did get to Oregon in the summer of '88, and he loved it. He was treated by the Blazers' physician, Dr. Robert Cook, and told anyone who would listen that the United States was a wonderful place. "He got Americanized in a hurry," Buckwalter said. "We might have gotten the deal done then, but the problem was that nobody knew exactly who in the Soviet Union could sign off on the guy. So things just stalled, and Sabonis went on to help the Soviets win the gold medal at the Olympics. I guess you could say that we inadvertently helped prepare him to beat the U.S. team, but what we also found out was that he could play against somebody like David Robinson and that he definitely belonged at the NBA level."

The Blazers certainly stayed on the case. Glickman made a trip to the Soviet Union in 1989 for another stab at signing Sabonis. Eventually, Sabonis did leave the Soviet Union, but it was to play in Spain. There was a disagreement about whether he needed surgery to solve the Achilles problem once and for all, and the Blazers are convinced Sabonis was given bad advice by people who stood to make a lot of money by shipping him off to Valladolid in the Spanish league.

"What you have now is Sabonis making big money

Tom Owens slams one home.

in Spain, playing physically at about two-thirds of his potential," Buckwalter said. "If he'd had the surgery and come over here when he was young enough, he would have been something special. But you have to say we took our shots at it."

There is a certain irony in the fact that part of the Sabonis story involved a leg injury. Certainly that was the centerpiece of Bowie's failure to become an impact center in the NBA, and there's no doubt whatsoever that the Blazers' post-1977 history began with the team's most famous foot problem of all.

Things seemed so beautiful for Portland basketball in '77. The Blazers followed up their championship season by simply laying waste to the rest of the NBA for most of 1977-78. Bill Walton played at MVP level, coach Jack Ramsay's defense-and-passing game was run to perfection and Portland zoomed off to a 50-10 start.

"We were playing right then as well as any team has ever played, I believe," Walton said. "We had teams beaten before we'd even tip off, especially in Portland (where the Blazers won a record 26 straight before losing their first home game of the season on February 12). It was a marvelous feeling to come to the arena and know we were going to win again. It was the same kind of domination I'd experienced at UCLA, except that this was against the best competition in the world. We were playing wonderful basketball."

Back-to-back championships—at the very least—seemed almost inevitable, but unfortunately, the dream began to unravel the first week of March 1978 when Walton aggravated a previous foot injury and required immediate surgery. At the time, the prognosis was that he would be out for about three weeks, and that he'd certainly be back for the playoffs.

Gross suffered a stress fracture of the ankle and missed the rest of the season. Lloyd Neal hurt his knee at the same time Walton went out. Larry Steele went down. Lionel Hollins missed time and so did Dave Twardzik.

Yet with the exception of Gross, the gang that won a title just a year earlier was expected back for the first playoff series against Seattle. Walton practiced with a noticeable limp, but everyone remained upbeat and

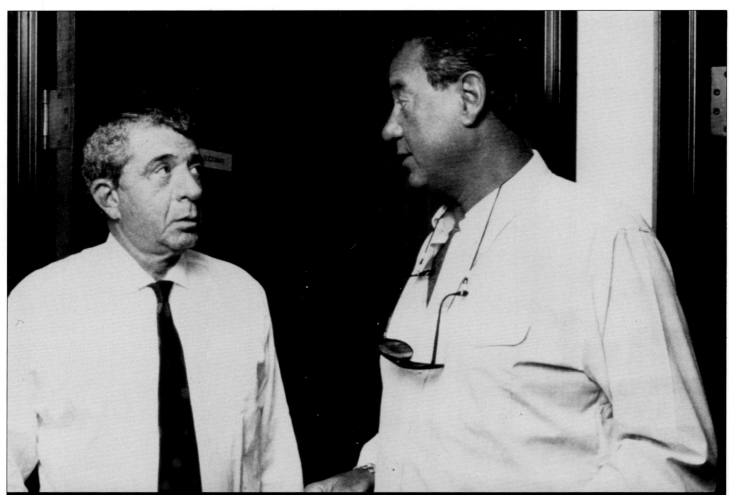

Bucky Buckwalter (right) vice president of basketball operations, talks with club President Harry Glickman about the team's 1988 efforts to land international star Arvydas Sabonis. Buckwalter was named NBA Executive of the Year in 1991.

"You know, the foot feels a lot better today than it did yesterday," Walton told a reporter just 48 hours after his surgery. "Who knows, maybe by next week I'll be running. I'll do just as much as I can every day and until I reach a point where I can play in the NBA, I won't play. When I reach that point, I'll be in there."

As it turned out, Walton wore a Blazers uniform just twice more in his career.

Portland staggered into the playoffs after losing 14 of its final 22 regular-season games and watching other players besides Walton drop like war casualties. Bobby

daily medical bulletins seemed to indicate he was recovering from what had been described as a nerve injury in his right foot.

Indeed, Big Bill returned for the playoff opener and managed 34 minutes despite obvious pain and limited mobility. He scored 17 points and collared 16 rebounds, but that was just about the last good news the Blazers ever would hear about their most famous player. The Sonics won that game in Portland, setting the stage for a 4-2 series victory, and then the boom dropped for real in Game Two.

The Blazers won it, 96-93, on a clutch jumper by Maurice Lucas, but Walton had hobbled to the bench in the second quarter. X-rays later revealed that he'd broken a bone in his left foot. He'd complained that both feet were bothering him after the initial injury and had taken a pain-killing injection in the left one prior to the second game—treatment which led much later to that dispute between Walton and the Blazers management.

The rest of the series was almost anticlimactic, as Neal also got hurt and the Blazers wound up playing on little more than heart and pride. Backup center Tom Owens was magnificent at times, Lucas and Hollins struggled to pick up the scoring load, but the young and hungry

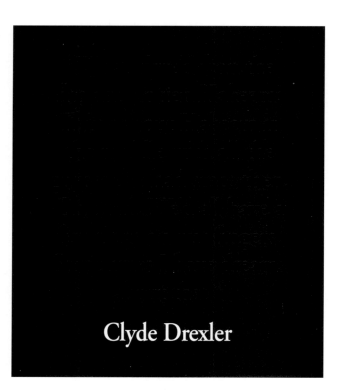

Clyde Drexler

Sonics were too deep, too tough and too healthy.

For all of that, the once all-conquering Blazers went down hard. They lost the fourth game in Seattle, 100-98, despite outplaying the Sonics—and then won Game Five easily behind Owens' 31 points back in Portland.

The Sonics finally closed the deal at home with a 105-94 victory, but both teams seemed to realize that the Blazers had proved a mighty point. "They were the defending champions, and played like it," Seattle forward John Johnson said. "They never quit. They were tough." And Ramsay saluted his troops in defeat, telling them to hold their heads high and announcing to the media that he had never been prouder of a team—including his 1977 champs.

"When we won the championship, we did it with a certain amount of class," Steele said, "Now I feel that we lost with a certain amount of class."

Most everyone in the Blazers family believed in the

Above & Left: Mike Schuler was the NBA's Coach of the Year in 1987 after guiding the Blazers to a 53-29 finish in his first year. He was replaced in the middle of the next season by one of his assistants, Rick Adelman.

Calvin Natt

Rick Adelman & John Wetzel

Jim Paxson

spring of 1978 that the first-round elimination had been something of a fluke, that wholesale injuries to Walton and so many of the key players around him had made the task of repeating impossible. Several players came right out and said they expected that Portland's place among the NBA's elite would be restored the following season when everyone got healthy.

They were wrong.

The wonder team was gone forever. Walton's foot kept him out the entire 1978-79 season, and that's when he began to squawk out loud about his medical treatment. Finally Walton announced that he wanted out of Portland and, prior to the 1979-80 season, he signed as a free agent with San Diego. Under compensation rules in force at that time, the Blazers were awarded two players—center Kevin Kunnert and forward Kermit Washington—along with a No. 1 draft choice for the loss of Walton, but the glory days were over.

"For a while, it was like we had a version of Camelot in pro sports," Weinberg said. "It was difficult to see it end so quickly."

However angry he might have been at the time, Walton now looks back at

Kenny Carr

able thing, and honestly, it's such a shame that it couldn't go on longer than it did."

One by one, the other Blazers from that magnificent team either broke down from physical ailments, moved on after contract difficulties or were traded in an effort to shore up weak positions vacated by someone else.

Boston guru Red Auerbach had made just such an eerie prediction to Blazers general manager Glickman shortly after Portland won the '77 championship. "Now it gets hard," Auerbach said. "Now they'll all think they're all-stars."

It was a prophetic warning.

Lucas fell out of favor during a strange 1979-80 season in which money matters—believing he was underpaid compared to others at his position—robbed Luke of the powerful, single-minded will to dominate that had been his Portland trademark. Eventually he was shipped off to New Jersey. Hollins, who was one of the most underappreciated players of his time, likewise got sideways with management and wound up being dealt to Philadel-

the end of his Blazers career with sincere regret. "We were doing something truly wonderful," he said. "We had a great coach who taught team-oriented basketball, and a group of individuals who believed in sacrificing themselves to be winners. That's really a rare and remark-

phia, where he infused some much-needed defense and ball distribution to the 76ers' star-laden lineup. Talk about unhappy times for Blazers loyalists: Lucas and Hollins were shipped off on the same day, Feb. 8, 1980.

Mychal Thompson follows the game from the bench.

Drazen Petrovic didn't start a game in his season and a half with the Blazers and averaged just 12 minutes and 7 points in the 95 games he did play. Those numbers are hardly noticeable in the statistical story of Portland's first quarter century. Drazen was selected late in the third round of the 1986 NBA Draft, Portland's fifth pick and the draft's 60th overall. (The Blazers had taken U.S. college players Walter Berry and Juden Smith, and international stars Arvydas Sabonis and Panagiotis Fasoulas ahead of him.) He joined the team three years later and was traded under less than happy circumstances in the middle of his second season.

Yet Petro, during his brief sojourn in Rip City, carved a fond niche in the hall of memories of Blazers players and fans alike. Many would list his enthusiasm for the game, his fiercely competitive spirit, his tireless work ethic, and his intense desire to excel among the intangibles that helped propel Portland all the way to the 1990 NBA Finals.

Fans will long remember the piercing eyes; the infectious smile; the Petro fist pumping the air after he or one of his teammates made a big basket; the seemingly effortless release of a three-pointer from beyond the circle, that storm-the-ramparts drive into the paint against all odds.

Already a star on the international basketball scene whom experts were dubbing a Croatian cross between a Jerry West and a Pete Maravich, Petrovic chaffed at his role on the Blazers bench behind established guards Clyde Drexler, Terry Porter and Danny Young. He yearned to prove his mettle as an NBA player after leading Yugoslavia to a silver medal in the 1988 Olympic Games, and a year later pacing Club Real Madrid of Spain to the European Cup championship. At the 1992 Olympics in Barcelona, Petro earned a second silver medal, this time with Croatia. Nine years earlier, at the age of 18, he had scored an incredible 112 points in a game in Europe.

Unhappiness with a lack of playing time eventually led to his being traded to New Jersey. In the two-plus seasons as a Net, Petro proved to the world that it was possible for international players to make it big time in the NBA. He led New Jersey in scoring for two years, averaging 22.3 in 1992-93, was one of the top three-point percentage shooters in the league, capping it all by being named third team all-NBA in 1993.

On a rainy stretch of a German autobahn outside Munich on June 7, 1993, Drazen's life ended in a fiery auto crash. He was 28 years old. More than 6,000 mourners crowded into the main sports arena in his hometown of Zagreb for the funeral. The Republic of Croatia had lost a native son and a national hero, international basketball and the NBA had lost one of its best young stars, and Portlanders had lost a favorite.

Postscript: In October of 1993, the International Basketball Federation (FIBA) and the National Basketball Association jointly announced that the Most Valuable Player Trophy for the McDonald's Open would be named in Drazen Petrovic's honor. The open is an annual tournament featuring club champions from five countries as well as a team from the NBA.

Kiki Vandeweghe

Steve Johnson

Terry Porter

Steve Johnson
was a sweet shooting
big man.

Kermit Washington

Kersey, Porter and Drexler in 1984

Steele's battered legs simply gave out. Likewise Neal's surgically-repaired knees. Gross succumbed to ankle woes, and Twardzik suffered a variety of injuries. In truth, the only physically sound Blazers standout off the '77 title team who departed while still healthy and on the proper wavelength with management was guard Johnny Davis—traded in the summer of '78 to Indiana for a draft choice that was used to grab Mychal Thompson. Holes had to be patched.

At one point during this wholesale dismantling of what was supposed to be a dynasty—remember, Portland was the youngest team in the NBA in 1977—University of Indiana coach Bobby Knight phoned his old pal, Portland player personnel chief Stu Inman, and asked mournfully if the day had come in pro basketball when it was no longer possible to hold any team together.

Perhaps the most amazing thing about the Blazers throughout the 1980s is that they never collapsed entirely. There were no truly disastrous years, although Ramsay eventually was dismissed in the spring of 1986. His hard-driving successor, Mike Schuler, lasted less than three seasons, even though he was named NBA Coach of the Year after going 53-29 in 1987-88. In all that time, the Blazers missed the playoffs just once—after they went 42-40 in 1981-82.

Former Blazers broadcaster Pat Lafferty, who kept detailed records and charts year by year, considers the 80s an interesting period in club history. "Look at the cycles most teams go through," Lafferty said, "and you usually draw a diagram that looks like the Golden Gate Bridge. Slow rise up to a peak, then down into a deep valley before the rise up to the next peak. It's happened to the Pistons, the Lakers, even the Celtics. But the Blazers never hit that valley. There were no really bad teams."

Ramsay's take on that decade is pretty simple: The Blazers kept bringing in enough good players to be respectable and sometimes even more, but never enough of them at the same time for serious championship aspirations.

The charismatic Thompson gave the Blazers seven decent seasons (16.7 points and 8.9 rebounds per game) and so did guys like Washington, Calvin Natt, Kenny Carr and Jim Paxson, a matinee-idol guard from Dayton who averaged 16 points over nine years.

The Blazers fell out of character only once in the mid-1980s, trading three very solid players—Natt, Fat Lever and Wayne Cooper—along with two draft choices to Denver for high-scoring forward Kiki Vandeweghe. They wound up getting plenty of points

Soaring above the crowd

from Kiki (23.5 average) through parts of five seasons, but that deal cut into Portland's depth and exposed weaknesses even as it addressed some others.

The bottom line always showed up at playoff time. After the championship of 1977, the Blazers only advanced past the first round twice in the next 12 seasons, and they never made it as far as the Western Conference finals.

"We always had the same problem—the Lakers," said Thompson, who was traded after the 1985-86 season. "But everybody else had the same problem, too. That was when the Lakers had all their great players together. We could push them hard, but we just weren't as talented.

"The most frustrating part to me was when we made the trade for Kiki. Here we were coming off a 48-win season, we had the second pick in the draft and there were several guys, like Calvin and Clyde, who were ready to take off. We could have been a really great team without the trade, although it would have helped to have a healthy Sam Bowie. But we had outside shooting with Jim (Paxson), good strength on the boards and great depth. If Calvin, Fat and Wayne had stayed, we might have been right there with the Lakers.

"I remember when they told me about the trade and said who we had given up for one small forward, I asked, 'Who did we get? Dr. J?' It was really a shame, because Portland and the fans were always so great, and we might have had another championship caliber team or two in there."

Paxson, too, agreed that the 1983-84 team—on which he averaged 21.3 points—could have been a breakthrough club. "After we won those forty-eight games in the regular season," Paxson said, "we lost a tough five-game playoff series to Phoenix, and the decision was made that we needed another outside threat. I had really been the only outside shooter. So they traded for Kiki.

"It was a tough call. The Blazers did get more scoring with Kiki, but with the guys we traded away, we lost our depth and some of our style of play. The result was that we still had some pretty good basketball teams, but we weren't deep enough. If you only went through the first six or seven guys, we were as good as anybody in

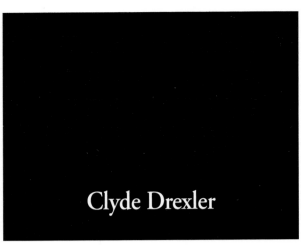

Clyde Drexler

the league. But the bench wasn't good enough, Mychal had to play out of position (at center) and there was always the Lakers if you got to the second round.

"I guess you could say those years were frustrating but we still played good basketball with exciting teams that worked hard. It was just that, after the successes of the late 1970s, an awful lot was expected and we never got quite that far."

The good news that came out of the mid-1980s disappointment, though, was that the Blazers made an organizational decision to return to their original philosophy; namely, that to become a true force again, they'd have to rebuild through the draft.

"We could see how the game was changing and what sort of players we needed to compete at the highest level," Buckwalter said. "Since we always had pretty good records, we knew we wouldn't have the luxury of drafting very high, so we concentrated on finding guys lower down in the draft who were good athletes. The theory was that we'd get players who had the physical ability to be great, then teach them more basketball skills once they were in the league. We wanted people who could run and jump, who would be suited for the high-speed, rebound-and-running game we felt we needed to play."

The rebirth started in earnest with the 1983 draft, when the Blazers stole Drexler with the 14th pick. A year later—lost in the furor over that Olajuwon-Bowie coin flip and the fateful decision to bypass Michael Jordan—Portland snagged Jerome Kersey with the 46th overall choice. In 1985, the Blazers' first-round pick (No. 24) was Terry Porter, who played forward at Wisconsin-Stevens Point but was projected as a pro point guard.

Move after move came up trumps. Slowly but surely, the larder was being restocked. Steady-handed Rick Adelman was given the coaching reins midway through the 1988-89 season and a return to prominence was truly afoot.

Soon enough, more banners indeed would be hanging at the Coliseum. Good teams somehow find their way back to the top, and the Blazers were ready once again to prove that they belonged in the NBA's upper rank.

By 1989, the time had come for Blazermania to hit fever pitch once again.

Kenny Carr

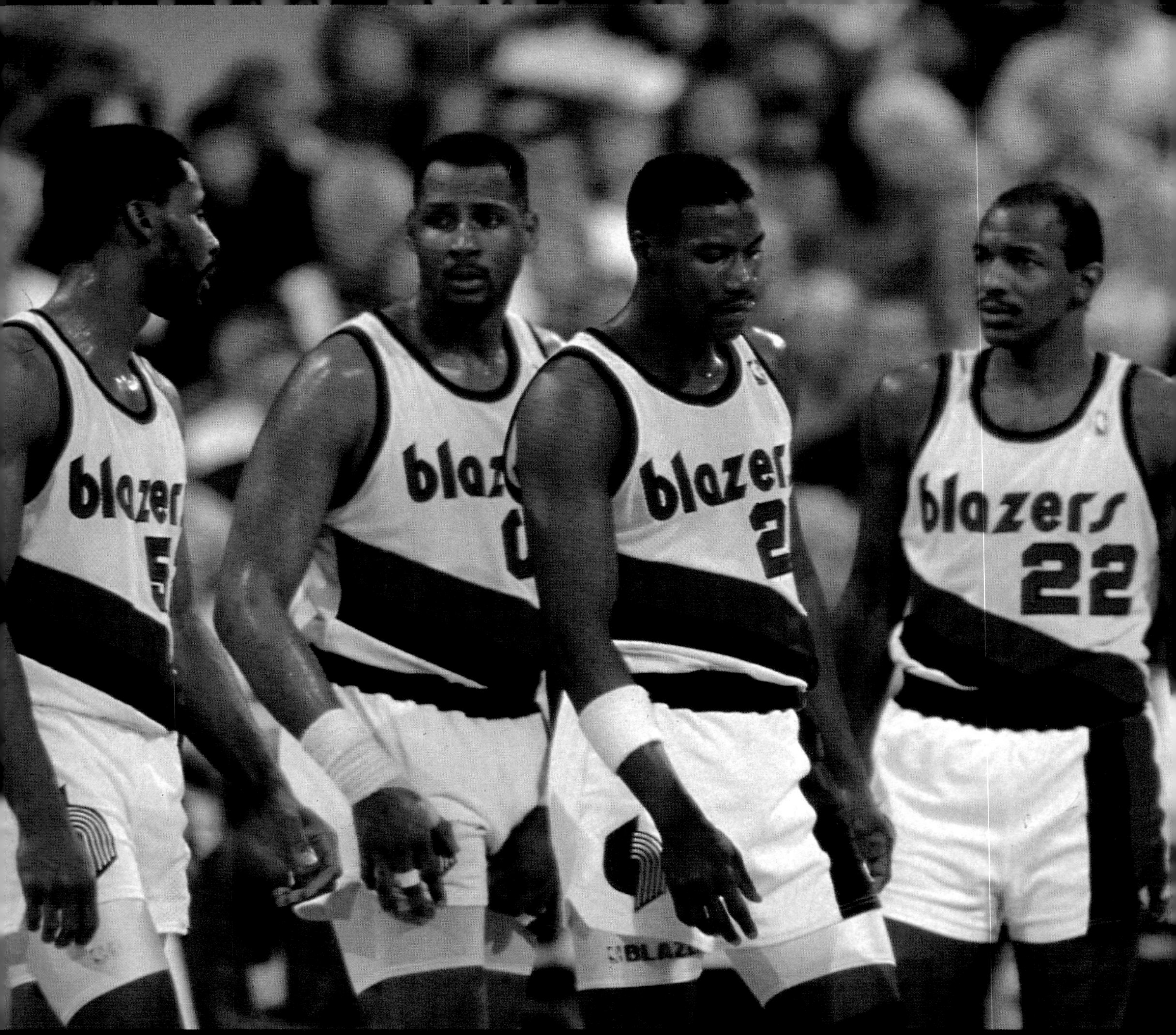
blazers
blaz
blazer
blazers
22

ALMOST, ALMOST, ALMOST

"*W*E HAD A HECK OF A TEAM. IN A DIFFERENT TIME OR DIFFERENT SITUATION, WHO KNOWS WHAT MIGHT HAVE HAPPENED."

—RICK ADELMAN

WITH ALL THE PROPER APOLOGIES TO CHARLES DICKENS, THIS IS A TALE OF ONE CITY.

CERTAINLY THE SPECTACULAR DOINGS OF THE PORTLAND TRAIL BLAZERS FROM THE FALL OF 1989 TO THE SPRING OF 1993—AND MAYBE EVEN INTO 1994—COULD BE CALLED THE BEST OF TIMES.

Over a five-year span beginning with an eye-opening run to the NBA Finals in 1990, the Blazers averaged 55 regular-season victories. They made the playoffs every year, captured two Western Conference titles, once posted a league-best 63-wins and played some of the most exciting, up-tempo, give-no-quarter basketball anyone has enjoyed since the days of the Showtime Lakers. These Blazers crashed the boards, defended like enraged pit bulls and dunked so hard they rattled rims across America. They were tough, relentless, hard-nosed and often downright thrilling.

Highlight-film stars like Clyde Drexler, Terry Porter, Jerome Kersey, Buck Williams and Clifford Robinson provided countless moments of exhilaration.

135

And there were good players around them, too—guys like Kevin Duckworth, Danny Ainge, popular veteran Wayne Cooper and later the explosive Rod Strickland. This gang was a joy to watch.

In 1992 alone, the Blazers battled dramatically into the Finals, then in the next couple of months saw their hometown host both the NBA draft—its first-ever trip out of New York—and the Basketball Tournament of the Americas, at which the sky-walking Drexler and his United States "Dream Team" mates began their wondrous run to an Olympic gold medal. Through the spring and summer of '92, Rip City seemed to have become the basketball center of the universe. Pretty heady stuff.

And yet if you listen to the Portland faithful—and they're not hard to hear—the whole affair of the early 1990s sometimes sounds like it was, if not the worst of

times, then surely among the most frustrating.

The problem, of course, is that the Blazers couldn't lug an NBA championship trophy out of it all. They became poster children for the phrase, "Close, but no cigar." In a city and state obsessed with hoops and devoid of any other major-league sports outlet, that one failure was exceptionally painful. These fans, after all, are the same good folks who judge almost any season against the Utopia of 1977—when Portland stood atop the basketball world.

Never mind that the deeds of Bill Walton, Maurice Lucas and friends took place back in the Carter presidency. That single championship lives on in Oregon, and sometimes it returns to haunt Blazers teams of other eras.

"When you combine such high expectations with the kind of day-in, day-out scrutiny that the Blazers come under in Portland, you've got a pretty tough task trying to make people happy," said Rick Adelman, who eventually lost his coaching job despite never enduring anything close to a losing season.

"We accomplished a lot of great things, and played very, very hard. We had teams that could have quit and didn't, guys who pushed it to the last drop in the tank. But the bottom line is that we never got our championship, and because we came so close, I guess the perception is that we should have."

Eventually, of course, even the hardest-to-please Blazers fans will look back on the Adelman teams as something very special, indeed. It's just that, when Clyde was soaring, Terry was bombing and Jerome and

Buck were banging the glass so hard that entire buildings shook, a championship seemed almost like their destiny. Three times, it was near enough to touch. The populace believed passionately that, doggone it, the Blazers deserved one. At least one.

The much-admired Cooper, who retired following Portland's discouraging loss to Michael Jordan and the Bulls in the 1992 Finals, tried mightily to put things in perspective. "Everything has to be perfect for you to win," Cooper said after Jordan and pals had closed out a six-game series. "I don't think anyone understands what a great run we've had. Frustrating? Well, I would think Phoenix (whom the Blazers beat in pulsating playoff series in 1990 and '92) would have to be the team that's frustrated.

"The expectations have been so high in Portland the past two years. I think they've been so high we didn't enjoy ourselves as much as we should have. We should have been sky-high. But every win was like a relief. It's not so much fun when you start putting pressure on yourself."

Williams, whose addition truly turned a good Blazers team into a near-great one, echoed those sentiments. "Winning a championship isn't something that just falls out of the sky," he said. "That first year (1989-90, when Portland won the conference title and then lost to Detroit), there was nothing expected of us. It changed after that. We weren't having fun last year

Buck Williams game in and game out draws the toughest defensive assignments and always delivers, even against taller adversaries such as New York's Patrick Ewing.

(1992). There was pressure from management and from ourselves. Every move all year seemed so calculated. You need to have fun. It was like every game was a playoff game all year."

Then there was the matter of an unhappy postscript.

You'd think the Blazers—after making serious title runs three straight seasons from 1990-92—would have been much appreciated, even loved by the home folks, and definitely given their proper due around the NBA. Instead, what they heard were accusations that they couldn't get over the hump because they really weren't a "smart" team, that they'd break down in critical situations, that all these gifted athletes went mentally soft when faced with their most serious challenges.

Adelman and general manager Geoff Petrie knew otherwise. They realized better than anyone else that the Blazers had limitations: lack of depth behind Porter at point guard, no shot-blocker to dominate the middle, not enough good shooters to complement their slashers in a half-court offense. Most of all, they understood that with the exception of the Western Conference finals upset by the Lakers in 1991, they'd simply been beaten by better teams.

It only added to the fans' frustration that the Blazers began to slip slowly backwards after that dispiriting loss to the Bulls. Injuries to Drexler and others crippled the 1992-93 team, which won the now-customary 51

"When Clyde was soaring...." Clyde the Glide, who has worn the Blazers' colors longer than any other Portland player, averaged 20.7 points in the 826 games he played over 11 seasons.

games but was dispatched by San Antonio in the first round of the playoffs. Then in 1993-94, Drexler came up ailing again for one significant stretch, several veterans showed they'd lost a step or two and the regular-season victory total slipped to 47. And once again, the playoffs came and went in a hurry—eventual champion Houston dusted the Blazers 3-1 almost before Memorial Coliseum fans could get warm in their seats.

The trend was duly noted and acted upon: Petrie resigned and Adelman was fired. Petrie later became general manager at Sacramento.

"There is no question that Rick is a good coach who did an outstanding job for us," owner Paul Allen said after the ax had fallen. "But sports isn't like other businesses. Sometimes you just have to look at the direction you're heading. If the chemistry doesn't seem right, or the direction isn't the right one, then you have to make a change. In fact, you owe it to the franchise and the fans to make a change if you believe you're getting further away from your goal instead of closer to it. They deserve your best efforts at winning, at being a champion. Obviously, we believe we have a better chance at directing ourselves toward that goal by making some changes."

Allen went after the best minds he could find for the transition, landing Seton Hall's highly regarded P.J. Carlesimo to coach the Blazers and hiring former SuperSonics executive Bob Whitsitt as president of basketball operations.

Common sense dictates that Whitsitt, Carlesimo and Co. arrived at a time when, by Portland standards, short-term expectations had been cut down to a reasonable size. The Blazers' slide a few rungs down the NBA ladder made it quite obvious that title aspirations might have to wait — at least awhile.

But the new brain trust nonetheless inherited a grand legacy from the Petrie-Adelman regime. NBA champions or not, those teams which often ran wild and produced so much excitement through the early 1990s left a tough act to follow. Bucky Buckwalter, who has seen most everything during nearly two decades with the Blazers, put it plainly. "A lot of work and some outstanding decisions went into the makeup of those (Adelman) teams," he said. "They were built on some good draft choices, trades and acquisitions. They were well-coached, and the character of that group was to play very hard, very tough basketball. We all have our work cut out for us trying to get back up to that level."

Buckwalter's assessment ought to be heeded. Likewise, those Blazers of 1989-94 that Adelman and his staff turned into one of the league's most feared teams deserve to be remembered more for what they accomplished as opposed

Former Oregon prep star Danny Ainge brought NBA championship savvy and a combative spirit to the Blazers party.

he Year 1992 could well be stamped, "Dream Year" in Clyde Drexler's scrapbook of memories.

EXHIBIT A: He was a first-team all-NBA choice after leading the Blazers to the NBA Finals against the Chicago Bulls. He averaged 25.0 points a game for the season, 26.3 points in 21 playoff games and 24.8 points in the six-game Finals series.

EXHIBIT B: He was runner-up for the NBA All-Star Game MVP honors after sparking the West to a 153-113 drubbing of the East. Clyde's All-Star game line included an all-time Blazers high 22 points on 10-of-15 shooting (including 2 of 2 from three-point range), a team-high nine rebounds plus six assists and two blocked shots. Clyde, who started alongside Magic Johnson in the West's backcourt, would have have been a shoo-in for the game's top individual honor had it not been for an even more sensational performance by Johnson. Magic, who returned to the court after announcing his retirement earlier in the season, scored a game-high 25 points (9 of 12 from the field and 3 of 3 three-pointers) and added nine assists in 29 minutes.

EXHIBIT C: Drexler was a member of the United States Olympic Team that made its debut at the Tournament of the Americas in Portland in June. Dubbed "America's Dream Team," TeamUSA, made up of a spectacular collection of some of the NBA's greatest players, went on to easily win a gold medal at the 1992 Olympic Games in Barcelona. Clyde was the fifth leading scorer on the team, averaging 10.5 points and 21 minutes while shooting .578 from the field. His teammates? Oh, Michael Jordan, Magic Johnson, Larry Bird, Charles Barkley, Karl Malone, Patrick Ewing, David Robinson, Chris Mullin, Scottie Pippin, John Stockton and Christian Laettner.

to what they did not.

OK, Portland, there wasn't a championship at the end of the rainbow. Not that time around. But step back a minute and enjoy the memory of that unique group which put some serious teeth back into Rip City.

The principal building blocks, obviously, were Drexler, Kersey and Porter—three stars in waiting taken in the collegiate drafts of 1983-84-85. Walter Berry of St. John's was a disastrous first-round pick in 1986, but the Blazers quickly wiped out their own mistake by peddling Berry to San Antonio that same December for Kevin Duckworth. Robinson was an outstanding second-round choice in 1989, and that same off-season, Portland unloaded oft-injured center Sam Bowie to New Jersey for Williams.

"I really believe getting Buck Williams might have been the key to everything we were trying to do," Buckwalter said. "Everybody knew he was a great rebounder and defensive player, but what changed things so dramatically was his presence, his attitude, his work ethic. With Buck around, it was so much easier to get all these other outstanding athletes to work harder, to commit themselves to improving their skills and blend together."

With Williams on board and all that other developing talent ready to burst loose, it seemed as though all the pieces fell into place at once and Adelman, who had replaced Mike Schuler in the middle of the previous season, was exactly the right coach at

Danny Young leads a pack of happy Blazers off the court at the Palace in Auburn Hills as Portland evened the 1990 NBA Finals series at one game each with a 106-105 overtime victory.

Clyde Drexler

the right time.

For instance, Schuler and Drexler had gotten onto completely different wavelengths, and there was no way Clyde—clearly the Blazers' meal ticket—would have blossomed so completely under the previous regime. On the other hand, the patient and even-handed Adelman had gained Drexler's confidence during Rick's years as an assistant coach. It was a perfect match.

"No question about it, we came together after Rick became coach," Drexler said. "So many things happened (the previous year) that we just couldn't get it together. But Rick's demeanor and competitive fire shows through the team. The team is a reflection of Rick."

And so, before the rest of the league knew what hit it, Adelman turned this new juggernaut loose. The Blazers went 59-23, a 20-win improvement, while logging a club-record 24 road victories.

The tone of the season was set early. The Blazers won their first two games at home, then took off on a typically dangerous three-game swing through Texas. They lost at Houston, then bounced back to win at San Antonio and Dallas. On that road trip, Portland had different scoring and rebounding leaders all three nights. The Blazers jumped off to a 12-3 start overall and never looked back. Their longest losing streak all year was three games.

Drexler exploded for a 23.3 regular season average and Duckworth established himself as a deadly medium-range shooter. He'd found the proper role with the right type of team. Williams and Kersey weren't exactly offensive machines, but they were ferocious down low where the NBA's dirty work gets done. And the mentally tough Porter by then had become a solid floor leader and outside threat at the point.

By playoff time, Blazermania was in full cry at the Coliseum and throughout Oregon. And yet no one really knew what to expect. After all, the Blazers had been bounced from postseason play in the first round each of four previous seasons.

Not this time.

Portland waxed Dallas three straight to get the party started in the opening round, then hooked up with San Antonio in a seven-game duel that, once and for all, gave this team a snarling identity that would last three-plus years. The Blazers and Spurs each held serve throughout the series, so the easy out would be to say Portland won it 4-3 by having the home-court advantage for that final game.

That summation would hardly do the series justice, since the Blazers' victories at the Coliseum in Games Five and Seven were both outright wars that were extended to overtime. The fifth game, in fact, needed two OTs before Portland survived 138-132.

Porter and Drexler combined for 73 points in that win, and Porter got his 38 by putting 54 minutes of wear on a very sore Achilles tendon. "Those two guys were unbelievable," Adelman said. "They raised their play to such a high level, especially Terry. He was dead out there on a sore foot at the end, but he made the plays all night. It's indicative of the way this team is, fighting through adversity."

After the Spurs tied the series in San Antonio, Blazermaniacs had to turn right around and go through the whole overtime agony again — and once more the Blazers hung on, 108-105, earning themselves a berth against Phoenix in the Western Conference finals.

A note about that close-out victory over the Spurs: After San Antonio won Game Six at home, guard Willie Anderson came right out and scoffed at the fact that his club had lost 12 straight games in Portland. "Forget about the home court. If we start off good against them, they'll fold," he said.

Anderson's challenge rankled Adelman, among others.

Michael Jordan and Clyde Drexler in a classic faceoff in 1992.

THE
PRIDE
THE
GLORY
THE
TRAIL
BLAZER
STORY

"I really believe getting Buck Williams (in a 1989 trade for Sam Bowie) might have been the key to everything we tried to do," said Bucky Buckwalter of building the teams of the early '90s.

Vinnie Johnson and Bill Laimbeer celebrate.

"Anybody who has watched us play this year, to say we'll fold, that's ludicrous," Adelman hissed. "They seem to do an awful lot of talking after they win a game. They're lucky we haven't had all our players (Duckworth had been out injured). I think it's time for them to give us a little credit."

Instead, the Blazers went out and earned it the hard way.

Drexler, who had been fighting a cold and flu-like symptoms, came out of a game-long shooting funk with the series on the line. Clyde scored 12 of his 22 points in the final four minutes of regulation and overtime, including five free throws in the final 26 seconds to nail down the victory. And in what would later become fairly typical of these outstanding Blazers teams, Portland won despite shooting 37 percent from the floor. Wicked defense down the stretch and a 60-48 rebounding edge did the job—a formula that would be repeated again and again over the next few seasons.

The conference finals were just as dramatic. Portland

won three home games against the Suns—by scores of 100-98, 108-107 and 120-114. The Blazers lost their first two on the road, but then closed out the series in six games with an incredible 112-109 triumph at Phoenix.

The Suns had arrived at the conference showdown simply brimming with confidence. "We feel we can beat anyone, anywhere," guard Kevin Johnson said.

But Phoenix never figured out how to finish the deal in a close game against the dogged Blazers.

It went like this: Duckworth's short jumper with 17 seconds left won the opener, then Porter canned a shot with 12 ticks remaining in the second game, capping the Blazers' comeback from a 20-point, second-half deficit. In Game Five, the Blazers scored the last seven points after being one down with 47 seconds remaining. And finally, in the clincher at Phoenix, the Blazers trailed 109-106 with 1:09 to play and proceeded to score the last six points—the back-breakers coming on defensive plays by Kersey and Williams, a block and a steal.

The Blazers' locker room in Phoenix erupts after the come-from-behind playoff victory that pushed Portland into the 1990 NBA Finals against Detroit.

After the Phoenix series, the Oregon media and even some national pundits were beginning to suggest that the Blazers were a team of destiny, one of those rare gangs that springs from nowhere, defeating all comers no matter what the odds. And perhaps the Blazers believed it, too, especially when they evened the NBA Finals at 1–1 by stunning defending champion Detroit on the road.

The scheduling format called for the next three games to be played in Portland, where the Blazers had won all nine previous playoff games — some in almost miraculous ways. "The Blazers have a tremendous comfort level at home right now," Phoenix coach Cotton Fitzsimmons said after his own team had been sent packing. "Beating them in that place is going to be hard for anybody."

Wild-eyed fans along the Willamette were talking about a three-game sweep at the Coliseum. And they saw one, all right, but the dream turned into a nightmare.

The poised, pushy, cocky and ever resourceful Pistons did the unthinkable. They stormed into Portland and won the series without even bothering to bring the stunned Blazers back to Michigan. Game Three was a 121-106 blowout that returned Blazermaniacs to earth and then Detroit methodically executed down the stretch for 112-109 and 92-90 grind-it-out victories that brought the whole wild ride to a sudden halt.

That third-game shocker seemed to turn everything around. The Pistons had lost 20 straight games at the Coliseum, a drought that stretched back to 1974. "If you're going to end a 16-year streak, this is as good a time and place to do it as any," Detroit coach Chuck Daly said. Maybe the Pistons had no right to feel confident, but they didn't shoot that way — guards Isiah Thomas, Joe

NBA Final's action vs. the Detroit Pistons at The Palace in Auburn Hills.

Dumars and Vinnie Johnson were on fire as Detroit made 16 of its 32 field goals from 16 feet and beyond.

Perhaps the Blazers' last chance to make a fight of the Finals came just at the buzzer in Game Four, after Thomas had hit a jumper and two free throws to put the Pistons up 112-109. Portland guard Danny Young unleashed a desperation shot from just inside the half-court line as time expired. The heave somehow swished through the basket, but it was ruled too late.

Just to make the Blazers' off-season a little tougher to take, the Pistons closed out the series by scoring nine straight points in the final 2:02 in the clincher, winning it on Johnson's jumper with less than a second remaining.

"In our wildest beliefs, we didn't imagine we would lose three straight at home," Drexler said by way of an exclamation point to the last loss. "Give Detroit credit. They were good enough. But we should still be proud of everything we did this season."

They were proud. They had a right to be. The Blazers' future seemed so very, very bright. And yes, it honestly looked as though there would be a championship out there sometime soon.

Confidence ran so high that books were commissioned on the Blazers' next two seasons, diary-type

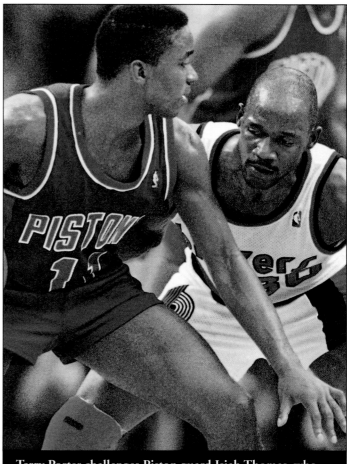

Terry Porter challenges Piston guard Isiah Thomas, who was the unanimous MVP choice for the 1990 Finals. Thomas had enormous roles in three of the four Detroit wins, including the series clinching 92-90 win in Portland.

inside peeks that are written with the realistic expectation that the team involved is going to win a title or come awfully darn close. Not many publishing houses are interested in the day-by-day account of a team that figures to go 20-62. But the literary world found Portland prior to the 1990-91 season, and Adelman agreed to keep notes for a book called The Long, Hot Winter. One year later, another publisher asked Portland sportswriters Kerry Eggers and Dwight Jaynes to recount the 1991-92 season in *Us Against the World*.

Mentioning the books seems relevant because it points out, first, that the people who publish things for a living realized that everyone in Oregon once again was hot to buy anything red, black and Blazered; and second, that the Blazers looked every inch like a team ready to win the great big trophy.

As everyone knows by now, Oregon malls got their supply of books, but the trophy never made it to Portland.

The 1990-91 season was full of thrills, but perhaps it is best summarized by a couple of numbers: 63, representing

The professional basketball career of Ramon Ramos came to an end on an icy freeway outside of Portland on a foggy December morning in 1989. The impression the rookie from Puerto Rico left on his team and the community, however, continued long after the life-threatening automobile accident replaced basketball with the daily rigors of rehabilitation.

Following a standout career at Seton Hall, Ramos earned a spot on the Trail Blazers' 1989-90 roster as a non-drafted free agent. His work ethic and affable personality made him an instant hit with his veteran teammates. His smile and against-all-odds effort to make it in the NBA made him a favorite with the Blazers fans. The 6-foot-8, 255-pound forward battled tendinitis during training camp and opened his rookie season on the Blazers' injured list. He was activated Dec. 6 but did not see action in the five games prior to the accident Dec. 16. The crash left Ramos clinging to life and in a coma for several weeks.

In the coming months the qualities that had formed the foundation of Ramon's life before the accident became more important than ever as he learned again how to talk, walk, perform basic living functions, and deal with the emotional challenges that accompanied his physical limitations. It would be a process that followed Ramos back to Puerto Rico nearly a year later, where his continued improvement now allows him to read and write in Spanish and English, and play casual basketball with friends.

While Ramos waged a battle for survival during the 1989-90 season, he was at the forefront of his teammates' thoughts through the regular season and into the playoffs. Several Blazers dedicated their season to Ramon. Amid the great pressure-packed drama of Portland's thrilling ride to the NBA Finals, Ramon's presence was an integral part of his team's all-important chemistry. By late May, he had progressed to where he was able to make a brief appearance at a team practice session. As he fought his own battles in private therapy sessions far away from the television cameras and Coliseum hoopla, Ramos' locker, complete with game uniform, remained in place, where it would stay the next season, and even the next. His rehabilitation eventually allowed him to return to Puerto Rico, but he remained in the hearts of the Blazers and their followers.

During the summer of 1991, more than 20,000 fans turned out to help the Trail Blazers raise $130,000 at Slam 'N Jam, an outdoor basketball and music event in Portland's Civic Stadium, for a trust fund to assist in Ramos' recovery. Players from throughout the NBA came to play in the benefit game. The loudest applause was reserved for the true guest of honor, Ramon Ramos, as he sat with his parents courtside. Ramon Ramos never played a minute in a regular season NBA game, but during a fabled period in the Portland Trail Blazers' 25-year history he cast an impression that left the team, and the community, forever touched.

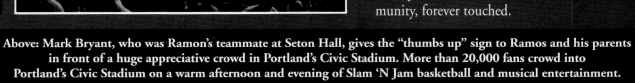

Above: Mark Bryant, who was Ramon's teammate at Seton Hall, gives the "thumbs up" sign to Ramos and his parents in front of a huge appreciative crowd in Portland's Civic Stadium. More than 20,000 fans crowd into Portland's Civic Stadium on a warm afternoon and evening of Slam 'N Jam basketball and musical entertainment.

Head Coach Rick Adelman and assistant coach Jack Schalow head a group of well wishers as Ramon Ramos makes his way to the basketball court on the infield at the Slam 'N Jam event in Portland's Civic Stadium.

Ramon Ramos, his father (with the microphone) and his mother (holding the large check) are surrounded by teammates, coaches and Blazers' front office personnel as the club presents proceeds from the Slam 'N Jam hoop and music fete in Portland's Civic Stadium.

the Blazers' franchise-record collection of regular-season victories; and 1, the number of playoff losses Portland suffered at home.

The first figure is significant because it established beyond a doubt just how dominant this particular Blazers team was, and also because it meant Portland would have that blessed home-court advantage for every postseason series.

And the second number?

Well, the Blazers lost just that one playoff game at the Coliseum—balanced against eight victories in front of the home fans. But the lone defeat, 111-106 to the Lakers in the opener of the Western Conference finals, turned out to be a season-crusher. The Blazers never could break through against the Lakers in L.A., and thus lost the series 4-2. It was another heartbreaking ending to a season filled with promise.

The most frustrating thing this time around was that the Blazers truly were a much better basketball team than they'd been the previous season. They'd added local hero and savvy NBA veteran Danny Ainge to the backcourt in a trade with Sacramento, and sleek, aggressive Clifford Robinson had matured into a powerhouse sixth man who could create hellish matchups along the front line.

Acquiring Ainge was a brilliant stroke for several reasons, even beyond his obvious ability to open the floor with long-range shooting skills. Ainge not only had won a couple of championship rings with Boston and was regarded as one of the league's feistiest, most combative players, he also helped loosen up a Blazers group that was generally pretty reserved. Ainge was a chatter guy—whether anybody else liked it or not. He might have caused some of his quieter teammates to roll their

eyes in exasperation a few times, but he also drew some—Robinson was a good example—out of their natural shells. And that turned into a plus.

The team couldn't be called perfect, of course. Duckworth still wasn't a shot-blocker, and problems with the half-court offense remained, but the Blazers could simply overpower most opponents with defense, rebounding and superior athletic skills. It would be oversimplifying matters to say that, once he'd gone over basic planning in training camp, Adelman needed only to roll out a basketball to get these guys off and winning—but even Adelman realized that a minimum of tinkering was necessary.

Adelman's most pressing preseason concern was for the front office to finish up contract extensions for Drexler and Williams. That got done on schedule, and right on cue, the Blazers reeled off 11 straight wins to open the season. By Dec. 18, they were 22-2. In those first 24 games, Portland was 8-1 on the road and rolled through one stretch of eight consecutive wins in which the smallest margin of victory was 12 points.

As the season rumbled on, the Blazers proved that they could turn up the defensive and rebounding heat on just about anyone—almost as though they were doing it whenever the mood suited them. Over one three-day span in March, they clamped down on Seattle and then the Lakers, wiping out a 24-point deficit to win one game and climbed out of a 21-point hole to steal the next—in Los Angeles, no less.

Naturally, there was wild optimism in Oregon at playoff time. After all, this was a Blazers team that had won 20 of 21 games to start the season and finished off the

Mark Bryant

year by winning 16 of 17. Nothing seemed impossible.

And for awhile, the script stayed intact. Oh, the Blazers got a little careless after winning the first two games of their best-of-five opening series against Seattle and let the Sonics get even. But the final game was in Portland and Adelman chose that night to make an interesting tactical switch: He'd had his guards play loose against the Seattle backcourt, which was filled with suspect shooters. Adelman realized while watching tapes of the Sonics' victories, though, that there was too much standing around on defense — so he decided to play Seattle's game. Challenge everything. Contest everybody. Be aggressive. Fly to the ball.

The result was a slaughter. The Sonics scored a bundle of garbage-time baskets to make the 119-107 final score respectable, but the game was a rout. And

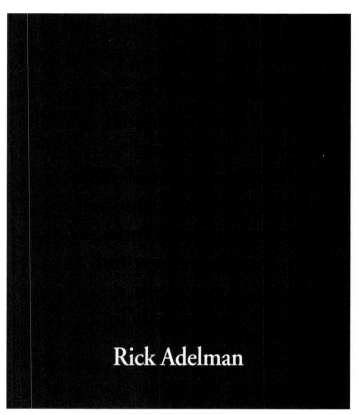

Rick Adelman

Adelman was pleased, not just that the Blazers had advanced to the next round, but that they'd turned up the heat and responded under pressure — the way great teams do.

Utah was next, and Portland blew out the Jazz 4-1. A couple of the Blazers' victories were close, including a 118-116 thriller in Game Two at home, but again, Adelman's big guns seemed able to step it up whenever the situation called for it. The series was never really in doubt.

Danny Young

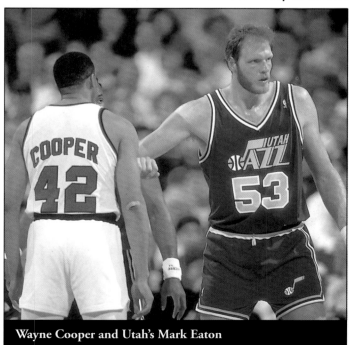

Wayne Cooper and Utah's Mark Eaton

153

The Blazers line up on the court before the Pistons game.

midseason pickup Walter Davis on the floor. Porter was being saved due to foul trouble and Drexler had indicated late in the third period that he needed a breather.

Adelman's take: "I didn't have a crystal ball with me. I didn't know we were going to be ineffective at the start of the fourth quarter. But we were. Everybody has talked all season long about how great our bench is. Well, if you can't use guys for two or three minutes and ask them to hold a 12-point lead, then our team doesn't belong here."

Whatever the cause, the effect was disaster. The Lakers reeled off 15 straight points almost in a heartbeat. Then, even with the front-line troops all in the game, the Blazers—though they took back the lead very briefly—could never regain a hold on things.

So the home-court advantage Portland had fought for all season was gone. In a striking parallel to that switch of momentum in the fourth quarter of the first game, the Blazers never got their home edge back. They held up in their other two tries at the Coliseum, but the Lakers won all three games in Los Angeles sending the Blazers home for the summer.

All of which led to that showdown with the Lakers for the Western Conference championship—and a shot at the Chicago Bulls, who finally were in the process of dethroning two-time champion Detroit in the East. Portland had won three of five from the Lakers during the regular season, but most of the games were close. And these, after all, were still the Lakers—58-24 record and all.

In his book, Adelman made a confident entry for May 17, the day before Game One in Portland: "People here get so excited about playing the Lakers, particularly when they think we have a chance to win. But I don't see them as any kind of test. I feel we've passed that stage as a team. We've played them and we've beaten them; we won the season series and the division."

One night later, it was obvious that the Lakers represented a pretty stiff test, after all. Not only that, but Adelman earned himself a serious media grilling after the Lakers rallied from a 12-point deficit entering the fourth quarter for their 111-106 victory.

The questioning concerned substitutions. It turned out that Portland opened the final quarter with Ainge, Robinson, Duckworth, Williams and

Terry Porter

By the time camp opened for the 1991-92 season, things had changed. But in this case, you truly could say most of the differences were cosmetic; for instance, Walter Davis had shaved his mustache. The Blazers had moved their training headquarters to nearby Lewis and Clark College from downstate in Salem. And the script on their uniform shirts had been slightly altered.

The players inside those jerseys, however, were basically the same. And why not, since the Blazers' core

Clifford Robinson

group had been within sniffing distance of a championship each of the two previous seasons and wasn't exactly a crowd of geezers. The message this time around was simple: We're good enough, so let's just get it right and finish the job.

They never did.

Once more, Portland posted the best record in the conference (57-25) and was a consensus choice of most national media experts to survive the preliminary playoff rounds and face off against the now-fearsome Bulls, who had roared through the regular season with a 67-15 record.

And that's the way it worked out, though not without some spectacular fireworks along the way.

Perhaps the strangest back-to-back games in Blazers history occurred during the first round of the playoffs—against the Lakers, naturally. Portland hammered L.A. at the Coliseum in the first two games—this was best-of-five—and intended to earn some much-needed rest by putting away the Lakers on April 29 at the Forum in Los Angeles.

That night turned out to be memorable, certainly, for all the wrong reasons. The Lakers won a 121-119 thriller in overtime, but the real story took place outside the arena. That was the infamous day that the verdict came down in the Rodney King beating case, and while the Blazers and Lakers ran and jumped and traded baskets, much of Los Angeles turned into a battle zone. Riots and fires broke out everywhere and, although activities at the Forum were not affected directly, huge sections of Los Angeles turned into frightening infernos.

"I'll never forget that night as long I live," said Pat

Jordan watches as Kersey slam dunks.

Lafferty, who was working the Blazers telecast. "I particularly remember the scene at the end of regulation. The crowd was going crazy over the game, the Lakers dancers were on the floor and the sound system was blaring out Randy Newman's song, 'I Love L.A.' The fans were singing along. While all that was happening, I looked up at the scoreboard and they were flashing messages about the rioting and which streets were now blocked off.

"It was almost surreal, like Nero's Rome. The city was burning down and the circus was still going on."

The Lakers' victory kept the series going, but when everyone realized the next day what had happened in Los Angeles, it became obvious that Game Four couldn't be played at the Forum. Eventually, both teams agreed on another site— the Thomas and Mack Center in Las Vegas, where the Blazers blew out the Lakers 102-76 on May 3.

With that bizarre series at last behind them, the Blazers hooked up with their old nemesis, Phoenix, and repeated the act that distressed the Suns so much in 1990. The Blazers ultimately won this rematch 4-1, but not before surviving a 152-151 double-overtime marathon in Phoenix—a game that players, coaches and staff on both sides claimed was one of the best playoff wars the NBA had ever seen.

There was irony in that Game Four triumph, too, since the pivotal play involved a jump ball that was called after several Blazers leaped on Phoenix guard Dan Majerle, who was lying on the floor trying to holler for a timeout. The call wound up beating the Suns, which

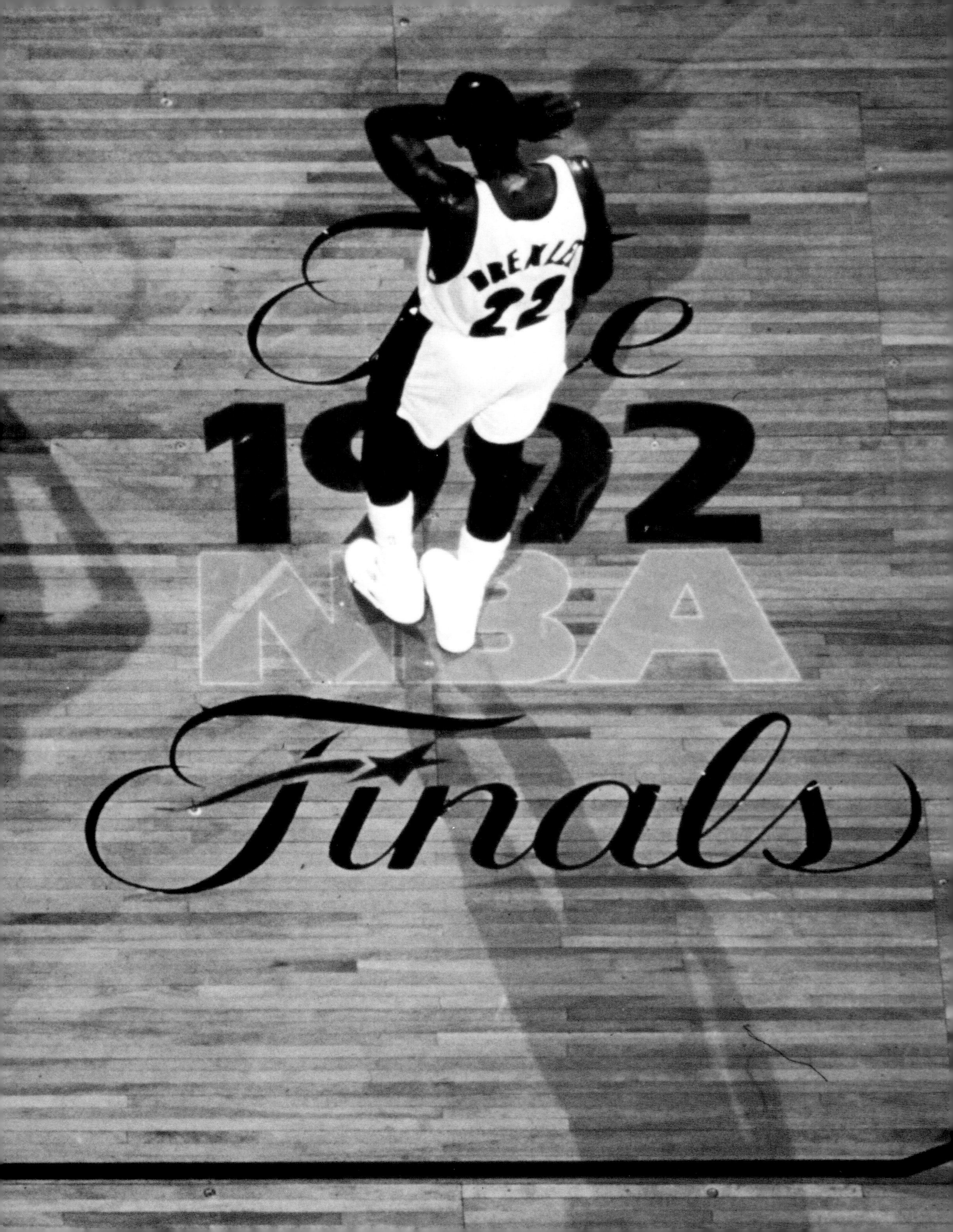
DREXLER
22
The
1992
NBA
Finals

only made the Blazers smile because they had complained all season about getting the short end of the stick from many league referees. The Blazers, who had been accused of whining about calls in practically every city in the NBA, at last could find amusement that somebody else felt they had been victimized.

Once the Suns had been eliminated, the Blazers again had to dispatch luckless Utah, and they did so by winning three times at home—what else was new?—and clinching with a breakthrough 105-97 victory at the Jazz' new Delta Center.

And so it came down to that battle with Jordan and the Bulls, in the series made famous in part when Michael got so hot that he scored 35 points in the first half of Game One—raining in six 3-pointers after attempting just 100 treys throughout the entire regular season.

Who can forget that image of Jordan, smiling, turning to the Bulls bench with his palms upraised as if to say, "Can you believe this?"

Just as they had against Detroit in the 1990 Finals, the Blazers could not perform enough magic at the Coliseum. They lost the third and fifth games at home to fall behind 3-2, then were eliminated in a sixth-game stunner at Chicago when they blew a 17-point lead in the final 13 minutes.

Buck Williams was so incensed at how the Blazers had come apart that he kicked a trash can in the locker room afterward. Drexler whacked it, too. The Blazers were not only done, they were angry and embarrassed. And heatedly blaming the officials again, to boot. It

Rick Adelman heads for the Blazers locker room.

was a horrendous way to finish their third straight magnificent season.

"It's devastating to lose anytime," Drexler said, "but to lose a game like this hurts even worse."

General manager Petrie, who would come under heavy fire less than three weeks later for failing to re-sign Ainge—who headed off to Phoenix—tried to sum up the feelings of the entire Blazers family the night of that Game Six debacle. "I don't think most people realize what a toll it takes on guys both physically and mentally when you get as far as we've gone the last three years," Petrie said, thinking of the players who'd battled the extra mile again and again without tasting champagne.

"Guys you used to know as bright-eyed kids look like guys coming back from eight years of war. They're grizzled, they've worn down physically, they have bumps and bruises...but they continued to push themselves as hard and as far as they could."

Adelman fought vainly to be upbeat amid the ruin.

"I'm very proud of every one of you," he said. "You didn't quit tonight. We lost because we flat-out ran out of gas. I'm not happy about that, and it hurts. But you did not quit, and I'm proud of you for that. We won't be champions, but you guys have the hearts of champions. You played your asses off. You had a great season, a great three seasons, and nobody can take that away from you."

And finally, Adelman said: "Our dream is not dead yet."

But sadly, it was.

Truly a Cast of Characters

"*W*ELL, YOU KNOW, I CAN GO TO THE HOOP AND
I CAN SHOOT OUTSIDE. HOW WOULD I PLAY DEFENSE AGAINST ME? HARD
TO SAY, HARD TO SAY."

—BILLY RAY BATES

TO LIVE IN OREGON AND NOT HAVE SOME CONVERSATIONAL
KNOWLEDGE OF THE BLAZERS, YOU'D ALMOST HAVE TO BE A CAVE-DWELLER.

AND WHAT A GROUP HAS BEEN THROUGH THIS GLAMOROUS FRANCHISE'S
FIRST QUARTER-CENTURY: ON COURT AND OFF, FROM HEROES TO FLAKES,
GUT-TOUGH STARS TO SIMPLY AMUSING BIT PLAYERS, HALL OF FAMERS TO
ONE-SHOT WONDERS, BILL WALTON TO CLYDE DREXLER TO...

Charlie Yelverton?

Perhaps it requires the true Blazers aficionado to remember ol' Charles, a
6-foot-2 guard out of Fordham University in New York City who averaged a
modest 7.9 points per game in 1971-72 — his only season in the NBA.

Yelverton, though, carved out a couple of notches in club history. Despite
everything you recall about Walton's once-radical politics, Yelverton was the first
Blazer to stage a one-man sit-in. And he also had, as far as anyone around the
organization can remember, the most dramatic reaction to Oregon flora and
fauna of anyone who's ever worn a Portland uniform.

The protest was sudden and eye-catching. It seems that Yelverton had become pals with Willie McCarter, another guard who played just that one year for the Blazers. McCarter was his buddy, his mentor, almost his big brother. So when the club waived McCarter at mid-season, Yelverton reacted with a remarkable fit of pique: He simply walked to center court at Memorial Coliseum one night and sat down during pregame introductions.

But Charlie's real passion was trees. He hadn't seen much more than a sapling or two while growing up in the Bronx, and the sheer lushness of Portland caught him totally by surprise. He kept pointing out how green everything was. During rookie camp at Lewis and Clark College, in fact, Charlie spent a lot of time between practice sessions just wandering the campus and gazing up at all the foliage.

Sometime later, Yelverton made an astonishing request. "I want to buy a tree," he said.

The assumption at that time was that Charlie intended to purchase a little seedling, perhaps, something he could transport back to New York after the season.

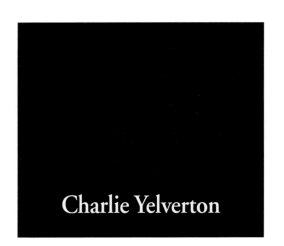

Charlie Yelverton

"No, I want one of the great big ones," Charlie said, referring to an Oregon Douglas fir. "I want to buy one and come back once in awhile just to look at it."

Blazers broadcaster Bill Schonely, however, insists that Yelverton wasn't the champion of the club's early crop of flakes.

"The craziest of all was Jim Barnett," Schonz said. "Jimmy was only here our first season, but in just that short time, he did so many nutty things, you wouldn't believe it.

"We're talking about a guy who would just curl up and lie down in the aisle of an airplane, or sleep on the luggage rack. I remember one game against the Lakers down at the Forum, Barnett just jumped on Wilt Chamberlain's back — jumped right on, like he was going horseback riding. He was about a third of Wilt's size, and the big guy threw him off and Jimmy went skidding along the court, almost the length of the floor. What a sight."

Oh, things like that are going to happen with an expansion team, you say. Sure, but the Blazers were a different bunch long after they'd become respectable — even once they were world champions. Some of the team's most visible stars were very, very unique characters.

Alaa Abdelnaby

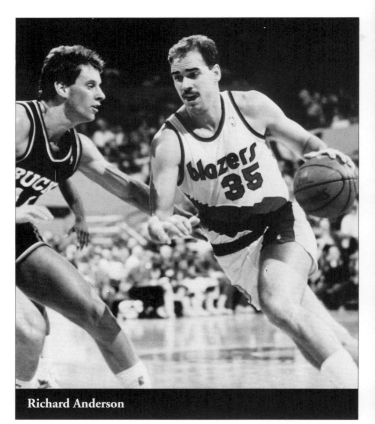

Richard Anderson

Charlie Yelverton

That list begins, quite obviously, with Walton.

You can argue that, when he was healthy, Bill Walton might have been the best center who ever played basketball. Assorted injuries cost Walton more than half of his entire pro career and left him hobbled for all but a couple of seasons, and still his impact was so significant that he was inducted into the Hall of Fame.

Yet Walton was unforgettable for reasons far beyond his basketball prowess—his only three truly productive pro years, after all, were 1976-77, when the Blazers won their title, his MVP season in 1977-78 and then 1985-86, when he captured the NBA Sixth Man Award on a championship team at Boston. The guy was brilliant when he could run and jump, but by his own admission, that really wasn't very often.

William Theodore Walton III, though, always managed to be different. For example, he was a shy superstar with a bad stutter when he arrived in Portland from his dominant days at UCLA. Given to commune life, radical political views and unusual eating habits, he was anything but a media darling. So what's the guy doing now that his playing career is over? Why, he's a

TV commentator decked out in coat and tie.

It's safe to say you couldn't have found a soul in Portland, even among his most ardent fans, who could have predicted in the early days how Walton's career might play out. Even Blazermaniacs who roared during the championship run of '77 probably guessed that Walton eventually would, say, wind up on a mountaintop in Tibet—perhaps chewing on a root and tending to a herd of sheep.

"In his seasons with the Blazers, Walton was unlike anything anybody had ever seen," said Schonely, who has seen them all. "You could find him sitting cross-legged on the floor in airports, burning incense, drinking out of a goat-skin pouch. Sometimes he'd carry around a paper sack with some kind of container of carrot juice. Put that with the beard, the weird clothes—I don't think he had more than two shirts—and the whole mountain-man look and the entire scene was just incredible."

It's almost a wonder that Walton wasn't run out of Portland, or that he didn't just flee of his own accord, long before everything fell into place on coach Jack Ramsay's amazing championship team in 1977.

Walton concedes that his initial disenchantment with the pro game throughout his first two years almost caused him to walk away entirely. In his autobiography, *Nothing But Net*, Walton wrote: "When things were at their absolute worst with the Trail Blazers—when some of my teammates hated my guts, and I theirs and their selfish, money-and-statistics driven style of play, when the fans and team management were unaware or not concerned that I had a broken foot and were accusing me of being a malingerer when I was hurt—I would

Onetime Blazers teammates and now broadcasters Bill Walton and Steve Jones share stories before the game.

call up the team owner (Larry Weinberg) in the middle of the night and tell him I was quitting.

" 'I hate this,' I would say. 'I hate everything about this. This is terrible. I can't do it anymore. I quit.'

"Then I'd hang up the phone, toss and turn the rest of the night, unable to sleep. By daybreak, I'd call him back and rescind the previous evening's announcement. I used to do this regularly: Get upset. Quit. Not quit."

But Walton followed that recollection with a statement that ultimately explained everything about his doggedness and his warrior-like demeanor once those on-court chemistry problems were solved: "Basketball and I were meant for each other. I always felt that the game was made just for me. It always came so easily, to the point that I thought I could do whatever I wanted to on the court—except stay healthy, of course—and not feel any pressure to have any other facets to the rest of my life."

Unfortunately for the Blazers brass, there most definitely were other facets to Walton's life in that era of Vietnam, protests and assorted other challenges to the once-sacred American value system.

First came the Patty Hearst issue. Walton's friend, Jack Scott, was a political rabble-rouser who was also in the sports business—athletic director at Oberlin College. There were rumors around at that time that Scott and his wife, Micki, had helped hide Hearst, who was then the country's most famous fugitive from justice. One media report surfaced that the Scotts had harbored Hearst at a rented farmhouse and, further, that their pal Walton actually had disguised himself and driven Patty from Oregon to Pennsylvania.

The flap around Portland was monstrous, naturally.

"The whole episode helped demoralize our club," Blazers boss Harry Glickman recalled of those difficult days. "I was up all night answering calls from newspapers and radio stations all over the country."

Finally cornered by some reporters on a road trip to Boston, Glickman snapped back. "Look," he said, "Bill Walton could shave his beard and trim his hair, but he can't stop being seven feet tall. You tell me you seriously believe he could drive Patty Hearst clear across the country and no one would have spotted him?"

Just when the Hearst escape rumors finally died down, Walton made the news again, and not because he was playing good basketball. Walton appeared with the Scotts at a press conference in San Francisco and said, among other things, "In closing, I would like to reiterate my solidarity with Micki and Jack and also to urge the people of the world to stand with me in our rejection of the United States government."

Jim Barnett

Well, now...

That sort of sentiment wouldn't play very well in Oregon under any circumstances, but the effect of Walton's bombshell was intensified because press accounts of his statement were taken a little bit out of context. Walton earlier had referred to "...the present government" of the United States, rather than the institution of government itself. That's really something of a

Billy Ray Bates was a brilliant comet who streaked—briefly—across the Portland sky.

different matter, but to some furious folks back in Oregon, semantics were hardly the issue.

"Mail poured in like an avalanche," Glickman said. "and the phone rang off the hook. If the media had quoted Bill's statement in its entirety, or if his clarifying statement containing the words 'the present administration' had been used in the first place, the Democrats, at least, would have applauded his remarks.

"It didn't happen that way, however, and it caused quite a commotion. We had calls from season-ticket holders threatening to cancel their orders unless we got rid of 'that lousy Commie.' But in all, we lost a grand total of eight seats.

"The only time I got angry was when they opposed his right of free speech. A couple of callers didn't even have the courage of their convictions. They canceled the seats in their company name but renewed them personally.

"The club issued a statement in response to what Bill had said. I told the letter-writers that I approved his right of free speech, even if I didn't approve of everything he said. In all, we answered more than 1,000 pieces of correspondence."

In time, Walton's political stands and even his association with the Scotts got pushed into the background just the way you'd expect—and the way Walton himself would have wanted it.

Basketball took over.

Just when things seemed as though they couldn't get any crazier, and the Blazers and their oft-injured center would never be able to find happiness together, the whole world fell back into place on the floor of Memorial Coliseum. Ramsay arrived, preaching the style of play Walton loved. Bill's feet, for once, did not betray him. Maurice Lucas, Dave Twardzik and Johnny Davis joined the roster all at once—and the sto-

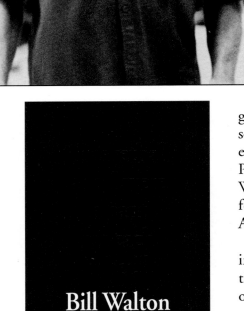

Bill Walton

rybook season of 1976-77 made the skies once more clear and sunny, even in Oregon.

Bill Walton spent just five seasons in Portland and yet—no offense to Clyde Drexler—you can argue that he was the most important, the most talented, the most talked-about and the most influential player in franchise history. Not to mention the catalyst for the team's only championship. There is no doubt whatsoever that his famous No. 32 belongs right where it is—retired and hanging in honor above the Coliseum floor.

There is considerable irony in the fact that the other five Blazers whose numbers have been retired in similar ceremonies were almost exact opposites of Walton—at least in terms of personality.

Geoff Petrie, the franchise's first-ever draft choice and later its general manager, was a prolific scoring guard through the team's first six seasons. Petrie was incredibly well-liked—even though he had conflicts with Portland's other star of that era, Sidney Wicks—and there was a bittersweet feel to the trade that sent Petrie to Atlanta prior to the 1976-77 season.

Petrie was almost the club's symbol in the early days, when contact with the public and appearances throughout Oregon were crucial in building a popularity base for the NBA in its newest outpost. Genial Geoff was the perfect man for that important role.

It's easy to forget that the Blazers weren't always the toast of the town. "When I first got to Portland," Petrie said, "I went to cash a check at a local bank and they didn't even know who the Trail Blazers were. I think they had to call and see if the check was real. That's what we started with."

More irony: Petrie was dealt away for the Hawks' choice in the 1976 ABA dispersal draft. Portland made the trade in order to snag power forward Maurice Lucas, the player who could truly complement Walton on a contending team.

Lucas, whose No. 20 now hangs alongside Walton's jersey, was a bundle of contradictions. Fiercely tough, competitive and almost perpetually scowling on the court—and sometimes off it—Luke actually possessed a kind soul and almost everyone who played with him considered the 6-foot-9, 218-lb bull a wonderful teammate.

There is no question about Lucas' value on the Blazers' great teams of the late 1970s. Yes, he seemed always to get his points and rebounds—the man was a

Calhoun to replace Maurice.

"Luke came out of the game angry. Assistant coach Jack McKinney approached Maurice in order to explain the defensive adjustment we needed to make. Luke refused to talk to him. The situation had reached a critical point. I motioned for Luke to come to me. I then did something I rarely do. I turned my back on the game in progress, and I gave my full attention to Luke. 'When I first met you this summer,' I reminded him, 'you asked that I treat you with respect. You said that I was the boss and that you would do whatever I asked as long as I treated you like a man. I've done that. Don't

Darnell Valentine

model of consistency that way—but more than that, he hungered to be a champion.

Ramsay believes to this day that one of the defining moments in the Blazers' championship season began with what might have been an ugly confrontation.

"It was a game against Atlanta and we were in a zone press after making a free throw," Ramsay said. "Maurice was out of position, a lapse I tried to remedy by signalling frantically to him to regain his proper floor position. He brushed aside my instructions with a 'Don't bother me' gesture. I quickly called on Corky

get mad at me. I'm just trying to do whatever I have to do to win this game. Now get yourself together and I'll get you back in the game.'

"I soon called for Luke to re-enter the game, during the remainder of which he played very well. We won going away. In the dressing room immediately afterwards, as was my custom, I called for the team's attention to begin my postgame evaluation. Before I could say a word, however, Luke stood to say, 'I want to apologize to Coach McKinney. I was out of order.'

"Maurice showed real strength of character in that

incident. He clearly established himself as a team man."

But Lucas somehow always felt threatened. Steve Jones, who has been around the Blazers since 1975, first as a player and then as a broadcaster, explained it this way: "With Luke, everything was turf. It goes all the way back to growing up in an environment where you had to establish your turf or somebody else would take it from you. He never lost that feeling."

Ultimately, Lucas' nagging belief that he was underappreciated forced the Blazers to trade him to New Jersey halfway through the 1979-80 season. Luke was still a solid player, but he'd worked himself into a near-destructive frenzy over the fact that he wasn't making as much money as some of the league's other power forwards. It wasn't the dollars and cents as much as the perceived slight that made Lucas a negative presence on that team.

Luke was still protecting his turf, and so he was—in effect—exiled from Portland. Fortunately, the whole saga had a satisfying ending when Lucas returned to the Blazers for his final season in 1987. And there was never any question about his worth on the floor—Walton often has said that no teammate, including Larry Bird in Boston, ever motivated him quite as intensely as Lucas.

The Blazers certainly have had their share of stars

Geoff Petrie chats with Blazers owner Paul Allen.

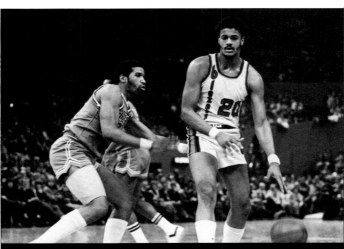

Bill Walton said that no teammate ever motivated him as intensely as Maurice Lucas.

through the years: Lionel Hollins, Mychal Thompson, Jim Paxson, Kenny Carr and of course, Kiki Vandeweghe, a scoring machine who could consistently light up arenas throughout the league. Nor should fans forget sturdy contributors in the mold of Wayne Cooper, who served two valuable stints with the Blazers and eventually moved his talents into the front office.

Later heroes like Clyde Drexler—now there's a uniform surely destined for the rafters—Terry Porter, Jerome Kersey and Buck Williams have given the faithful countless thrills.

And still, those other three retired numbers belong to Larry Steele, Lloyd Neal and Twardzik—hard-nosed, blue-collar players who fought through injuries and less than All-Star talent limitations to become essential components on some outstanding teams. Neal was hurt so many times that he earned the nickname "Ice"—a reference to the fact that he almost always had an ice pack on one or both of his legs after another night's war.

Twardzik was one of a kind. He seemed too short and slow to be an effective NBA guard, but the guy had deceptive moves, an uncanny ability to get a team into its offense and no regard whatsoever for his own well-being when he attacked the hoop—which was all the time.

"We all started calling him 'Pinball' because of the way he'd get bounced around by everybody on the court when he started to drive," Schonely recalled. "David had this hell-bent way of playing that was just infectious. It was impossible not to love him, but he was also a heck of a lot better player than most people thought he was. You had to see David night-in and night-out to appreciate what he brought to a team, which was a lot.

"For all the great players that have come though Portland, I wouldn't be surprised if a lot of fans still consider David their favorite. He'd be a great choice."

But not the only candidate.

dispirited—not to mention battling with San Diego for the conference's final playoff spot.

Bates came out of nowhere, it seemed, and he hit like a nuclear weapon. Here was an unpolished diamond, a 6-foot-4, 210-pound bundle of natural talent which never had been refined. Billy Ray grew up in rural Mississippi where he'd picked cotton as a kid, eventually played ball at Kentucky State and then drifted off into the Continental Basketball Association with a team called the Maine Lumberjacks.

That sort of background was perfect for the Blazers ace scout Bucky Buckwalter, who always was off comb-

Lionel Hollins

For all the Waltons, Lucases, Drexlers, Porters—and even the Twardziks—that have brought Coliseum crowds up and cheering, one guy Blazers fans never will forget played less than three seasons in Portland, and yet his memory remains as though in permanent freeze-frame.

Billy Ray Bates.

There was an air of something close to desperation when Billy Ray exploded onto the scene late in the 1979-80 season. That was the year both Hollins and Lucas had been traded in February after long contract hassles. The Blazers were undermanned, hurting and

ing odd spots looking for untapped talent, players who somehow had slipped through the cracks. And when Bucky saw Billy Ray Bates, he could scarcely believe his eyes. "You can look and look and look, and maybe never come across a kid with his body and those kinds of skills," Buckwalter said. "He was raw, undeveloped, and bursting with talent."

When Blazers personnel chief Stu Inman contacted Mike Uporsky, Billy Ray's coach in Maine, he asked: "Mike, is he the best in your league?" Uporsky quickly replied, "Stu, he might be the best in your league. Only

Lucas, whose No. 20 now hangs alongside Walton's jersey, was a bundle of contradictions. Fiercely tough, competitive and almost perpetually scowling on the court, Lucas possessed a kind soul and was universally considered a wonderful teammate.

Paul Westphal has more natural ability. I'd get him on a plane before anyone else finds out."

Unfortunately, Billy Ray wasn't exactly an easy sell on a coach like Ramsay, a man who treasured fundamentals, sound positioning, team concepts and tightly focused play. If the Blazers weren't truly aching for a shot of pure adrenalin, even the rave reviews of Buckwalter might not have gotten Billy Ray a look. Some help was needed, though, and here it was—unproven, undisciplined, but also undeniable.

"You can't even imagine the effect that Billy Ray Bates had on our basketball team," Schonely said, remembering those first few electric evenings. "He joined us on a road trip at Madison Square Garden in New York, and by the time we got back to Portland, he was already a legend. It was that dramatic."

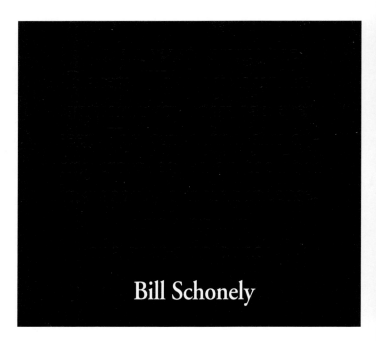

Bill Schonely

Bates was an innocent in the ways of the world—not to mention the conventions of the NBA. He had almost no experience in big cities and certainly none in structured, big-time basketball. Billy Ray once asked Blazers trainer Ron Culp, quite seriously, how it could be that there was snow at the top of Mount Hood, but none down at the bottom.

But what a player.

Ramsay was hesitant to use Billy Ray except in emergency

Mychal Thompson

Mychal Thompson has fun helping a young fan learn about dunking.

Kenny Carr

Thompson posts up between NBA greats Julius Erving and Moses Malone.

Kiki Vandeweghe, a scoring machine
who could light up any arena in the league.

Wayne Cooper served two solid
stints with the team, and later
moved into the front office.

Larry Steele played his entire professional career—nine years—in Portland. His aggressive defense—he led the league in steals one year—also made him the team's all-time leader in disqualifications.

Lloyd Neal, a 3rd round pick in the 1972 draft out of Tennessee State, played a major role in the team's 1977 championship. At just 6-foot-7, he started at center for two years in the pre-Bill Walton days.

situations, which meant that Portland most likely was taking a licking and needed points by the bushelful. Quickly. Bates then simply took over, crashing to the basket for thunderous dunks, pouring in jumpers from all points of the compass—in short, playing one-on-one basketball but with so much ability that everyone else on the floor seemed to disappear. One night in Chicago, he scored 16 points playing just part of the fourth quarter.

Bates also amazed everyone with his instinctive feel for the game and a tremendous ability—with his huge hands—to pass in traffic. Bobby Gross, who was a maestro at delivering the ball to open teammates, admitted he was impressed. "I don't know if he can play in a pattern," Gross said, "but he's good, isn't he? Something special."

One night near the end of the regular season, Bates scored 22 points in a win over Golden State that the Blazers badly needed. He was asked afterward about a key play on which he'd driven to the basket. "Well, I knew I could beat the old guy," Billy Ray said. "What old guy?" a reporter asked. "You know, the old guy who used to play for Boston," Billy replied.

He was describing Jo Jo White, who was all of 33.

"You just had to see Billy Ray to believe him," Schonely said. "He had charisma, and his body—he looked like he was chopped from granite. The things he did were phenomenal and the fans in Portland went crazy over him. He won a game one night by just grabbing this long pass in a crowd near the basket and just jumping up over everybody and dunking the thing. The place was a madhouse when he did that.

"To this day, the Blazers get calls saying, 'Bring back Billy Ray Bates.'"

Perhaps predictably, Billy Ray was a shooting star in more ways than one. He averaged 12.3 points in 168 games for the Blazers, but that figure is a bit misleading because he played only 18 minutes per game.

Eventually, the Blazers waived Bates following the 1981-82 season. "It was kind of sad because he was so unspoiled when he came to Portland, but there was no way a guy like that was ready to handle fame and money and all that," Schonely said. "He just couldn't cope with it."

The saga of Billy Ray Bates still casts its shadow, however. As The Schonz says, Portland fans have never forgotten him—or the pure, unadulterated excitement he brought to town at a time when the franchise needed him most.

But then, in some ways that's the story of the Trail Blazers and all the remarkable individuals who've come along to leave their mark. It's been an entertaining group—and more often than not, a winning one.

Background and inset right:
Dave Twardzik, fiesty, slick and tough.

AND NOW, ANOTHER PALACE

"*T*HIS IS A STRONG FRANCHISE, NOT ONE THAT HAS TO BE COMPLETELY REBUILT. OUR GOAL IS TO RETURN THIS TEAM TO THE ACCOMPLISHMENTS OF 1977."

—P.J. CARLESIMO

THERE IS AN OLD SAYING THAT HISTORY TENDS TO REPEAT ITSELF. IF THAT IS TRUE, THEN THE PORTLAND TRAIL BLAZERS HAVE EVERY REASON TO EXPECT A SECOND QUARTER-CENTURY EVERY BIT AS SATISFYING AS THE FIRST.

"OUR FANS HAVE GOTTEN USED TO EXCITING TEAMS, WINNING TEAMS," OWNER PAUL ALLEN SAID. "THAT'S A COMPLIMENT TO ALL THE GREAT PEOPLE WHO MADE THE BLAZERS SUCH A SUCCESS STORY, AND WE HAVE EVERY INTENTION OF UPHOLDING THAT TRADITION. WE WANT TO WIN— AND WIN CHAMPIONSHIPS—AS BADLY AS EVER, AND WE'LL DO WHATEVER IT TAKES TO GET THAT DONE."

Allen, who made billions in the computer software business and bought out previous Blazers owner Larry Weinberg in 1988, made some dramatic moves following what was perceived—at least in Portland, the NBA's high-rent district—as a disappointing 1993-94 season.

Coach Rick Adelman, who guided the Blazers through three consecutive runs at the league title from 1990-92 and never had a losing season, was dismissed in favor of dynamic P.J. Carlesimo, who was one of the hottest commodities in college coaching. Carlesimo turned around a once-moribund program at Seton Hall, molded his team into a perennial national powerhouse and took the Pirates to the NCAA Final Four in 1989.

The spot at the top of the Blazers' basketball organizational chart changed hands, too. Geoff Petrie, senior vice president of operations, resigned and was replaced by another young go-getter, 38-year old Bob Whitsitt—who was named NBA Executive of the Year for his work with the Seattle SuperSonics. Whitsitt was installed as president in charge of the basketball operations, while marketing whiz Marshall Glickman, son of Blazers founder Harry Glickman, became president on the business side.

It's hard to imagine any organization—in pro sports or anywhere else—undertaking such a shakeup, especially

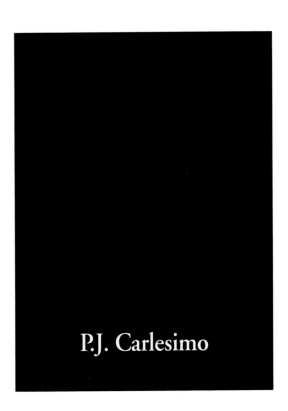

P.J. Carlesimo

since the Blazers weren't exactly scuffling. Portland had missed the playoffs just once in 18 seasons, none in the previous 12, and fiscally, times were good. The club simply continued to build on its record string of sellouts at Memorial Coliseum, a streak that started in 1977, and a following that had the team leading the league in local television ratings for 15 straight seasons.

A study done by *Financial World Magazine* estimated the value of the Blazers franchise at $122 million in 1994, a giant leap up from $84 million just a year before and fifth-highest in the NBA behind the Los Angeles Lakers, Detroit, New York and Chicago—huge markets, every one of them.

But Allen made a fortune as a founding partner in Microsoft back in the 1970s by looking into the future instead of reacting to events in the present. Clearly he was seeking to leap-frog into a new era with the Blazers

Bob Whitsitt, 1994 NBA Executive of the Year, answers questions at a news conference on July 12, 1994, when his appointment as president and general manager of Blazers Basketball is announced.

Rod Strickland

Owner Paul Allen is a self-confessed basketball junkie and an incurable Blazers fan.

and beat the competition once again.

Allen already had seen one dream come true—not just for the Blazers, but for the city of Portland and the entire state of Oregon. Despite a raft of predictable objections and difficulties along the way, he won a tough battle to begin construction on a new multi-purpose arena complex adjacent to the Coliseum—and do it in partnership with the city. The fabulous Rose Garden, with its 20,000-plus seats and more amenities than a Blazers fan could possibly imagine, will open for the 1995-96 season.

"There were a lot of great things to look at when I actually got the coaching offer in Portland," Carlesimo said. "Obviously, it's a solid franchise in a wonderful place, with outstanding ownership totally committed to winning. But the new building was an exciting plus. Think of what it will be like to move into the Rose Garden in a couple of years. What a thrill that will be for everyone. It's tough to ask for more than that."

Ah, the Rose Garden.

The name ought to be enough, just on the face of it. "I realize it can have a couple of meanings, and they both fit," Allen said after months of speculation about what the new edifice might be called. "We had all sorts of suggestions and ideas, but it's funny—the Rose Garden was the first name that popped into my mind back at the beginning. The longer we went along, the more it seemed that that first thought was maybe the best one."

Yes, yes, members of the media from all over the United States soon will be able to attend events in Portland and deliver witty lines like, "They never promised us a Rose Garden, but..."

Expect so many variations on that theme that the average Portlander may wish the city could switch its floral symbol to the orchid or perhaps even a blue spruce. Anticipate, also, that reporters whose teams get thumped by the new-look Blazers sometime soon will make reference to finding thorns in the Rose Garden, etc.

Eventually the locals will learn to just shake their heads

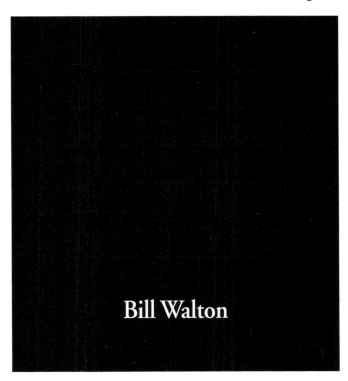

Bill Walton

or roll their eyes, much the way they've come to handle all those supposedly clever references to the area's rainfall.

Down deep, Oregonians will be able to smile and think: You wish you had this palace back home. And what a piece of opulence it should be.

Naturally, every convenience and new-fangled, customer-friendly addition was built into the plans for the Rose Garden, which costed out at $262 million.

Streets are being redesigned for easy access, ample parking will be provided and even the public transportation system will be integrated into an overall plan—just to make it easier for the public to enjoy its new playground. And at every step from discussion to laying concrete, the task force working under the umbrella of the Oregon Arena Corporation made sure every environmental concern was addressed.

Jo Allen Patton, the owner's representative for OAC, kept a close watch from conception to construction—always making sure the partnership the Blazers struck with the city of Portland was being honored on every count.

Marshall Glickman insists the Blazers were adamant from the outset that, sure, they wanted a new arena, but that they wanted to build it in cooperation with the people of Portland—instead of forcing it down anyone's throats.

"We never wanted to cause the execution of the Coliseum," he said. "That was foremost. The next thing is that most sports ownership groups want to extract money from the taxpayers, and they do it by threatening to leave town. That was three billion miles from what we wanted. We said from the beginning that the team wasn't going anywhere. We wanted to create a task force with the city that would solve almost every concern—after all, these people are our neighbors. Not just in a corporate sense, but in the real world. Some of them live right up the street.

"We're going to have a partnership that will make money—real money, not that phony-baloney stuff you hear about all the bucks a new building might bring into town. We plan to work with the city and operate the Rose Garden in a way that makes a profit for us and for Portland.

"Let's face it. We're not just in the basketball business anymore. Sure, that's still the No. 1 priority and it's what got us into headlines in the first place. The ball club is what put the spotlight here. But there's a limit on revenue you can generate from just basketball, so we're really in the entertainment business now. That's a much wider spectrum, and it brings up all sorts of exciting possibilities."

No effort or expense has been spared, it seems, to make the Rose Garden a national, even worldwide, showplace for all sorts of events.

As Marshall Glickman indicated, however, basketball remains the centerpiece. Fans may be delighted to hear about a "state-of-the-art" arena, but first of all they want to know what this fellow Carlesimo has in mind, how Whitsitt's wheeling and dealing — so creative in Seattle — fits into the picture, who's coming, who's going, and what they can expect from, say, Aaron McKie, the Blazers' most recent first-round draft choice. They want to know when they can start catching championship fever again, when the phrase "Rip City!" will be ringing in people's ears around the time of the NBA Finals.

Allen feels the same way.

After all, the owner is a self-confessed basketball junkie who purchased the Blazers because he'd become an incurable fan. One story Allen has pretty much kept to himself for a few years offers a nice insight into the enthusiasm of this ultra-rich gentleman who pretty much holds the Blazers' future in his hands.

It's best to let Allen tell it: "Fairly soon after I bought the team, it became obvious there were some difficulties with our coach, Mike Schuler. Conflicts between Mike and some of our key players had come up. Clyde Drexler and Kiki Vandeweghe came to my house to discuss the entire situation.

"Well, I've got a basketball court outside and it happens to be lighted, so you can actually shoot around a little bit at night. Clyde asked me if I really played on it, and I said I did once in awhile, and so then he asked me if I had a basketball.

Paul Allen

"What happened is that the three of us wound up out on this court, late at night, playing a game of H-O-R-S-E. You have to know that it was raining that night, too, so here I am out in the dark with these two superstars on my new team, fooling around, and the ball would go bouncing off toward some bushes and Clyde's hopping over things to chase after it. I had visions of Clyde or Kiki breaking an ankle or something. How would that have looked? 'Crazy Owner Injures Superstar.'

"Anyway, I think they let me win. We were just shooting jump shots. And what I remember most about it is that my last shot, the one to win the game, was this thing kind of from behind the backboard. And I had to look right into a floodlight. So it was into the lights, into the rain, over the backboard — nothing but net. Just like those commercials with Michael Jordan and Larry Bird.

"I realize these guys are great athletes and the whole thing about shooting around in the middle of the night sounds kind of crazy, but after all, basketball is still a game. And it's a great game. And yes, it's a game that I want the Blazers to win.

"I know our fans are hurting when we lose, especially at the end of a season when we lose in the playoffs and it's all over. That's just such an empty feeling. I can appreciate how the fans feel, because one thing Larry (Weinberg) told me was how much it would hurt when that happened. He was right. He said you'll find yourself thinking: Another day will come, we'll have another chance, the world will be fine. But right at the moment when you look up at that scoreboard and then go see the looks on your players' faces and see that pain, all the reassurances about a brighter day tomorrow don't make it hurt any less.

"Believe me, nothing helps."

Which is why Allen and his new basketball brain trust went right into high gear trying to re-establish the Blazers as an NBA force. Not just a good team, but a great team. One of the first things Carlesimo did was ask people around the office where he could find a really great picture from the 1977 championship season — a shot that captured the essence of that sensational victory. P.J. wants to have the thing blown up to mural size for his office wall as a reminder to one and all that everyone's goal is not just making the playoffs. It's winning another NBA title.

Carlesimo and Whitsitt have come aboard at an interesting time in Blazers history. Certainly they're following a tough act — the teams put together under the stewardship of Petrie and Adelman never won less than 47 games, never missed the playoffs, twice won Western Conference championships. And yet the usually impossible expectations of the Portland faithful actually were tempered a bit after a first-round playoff loss to Houston in '94.

"People that are waving for that championship banner for next season better take it down the flagpole a little bit," he said.

By all accounts, the Blazers have constructed an impressive basketball hierarchy. Whitsitt and Carlesimo arrived with different but spectacular qualifications, and they teamed up immediately with player personnel specialist Brad Greenberg and scout Bucky Buckwalter to begin whatever overhaul the club might need.

Carlesimo admitted he was impressed with Allen's full-bore approach to restructuring the entire

P.J. Carlesimo gets his first taste of coaching at the professional level during the Rocky Mountain Review, a rookie summer league held in Salt Lake City.

Reality hit home, even in Oregon.

Despite having a solid nucleus of battle-tested veterans and some bona fide stars remaining from those teams of the early 1990s, the Blazers found themselves in a transition mode. Whitsitt went so far at his introductory press conference to caution fans against being overly optimistic—at least for the short term.

organization. "We hired the NBA Executive of the Year," P.J. said. "I talked to a lot of people I know and I heard 100 percent positive back about him. With Bob Whitsitt and Brad, I'm sure 26 other teams in the league will look at this and go, 'Whoa, Portland's pretty serious.' "

Yes, that much is obvious—which puts Carlesimo

Wally Scales, vice president, special events, and Marshall Glickman, president, were the recipients of a recognition award from the Northeast Community Development Corporation (NECDC) for the Blazers' and Oregon Arena Corporation's commitment in helping revitalize northeast Portland and assisting in the effort to provide affordable housing to low income families.

into a pretty bright glare. Even armed with a five-year contract, Whitsitt's canniness at acquiring key personnel and Allen's considerable financial resolve, Carlesimo still begins his Portland tenure as a 45-year old coach with no NBA experience other than a stint as an assistant with the "Dream Team" during the '92 Olympics.

Before P.J. had so much as conducted a single Blazers workout, however, plenty of people who know the NBA lined up to suggest that Allen had found himself a good one.

"A very knowledgeable basketball guy," former Detroit and New Jersey coach Chuck Daly said of Carlesimo. "Style of play? He's like all of us. Pat Riley was 'Showtime' in L.A., but it's 'Uglyball' in New York. It pretty much depends on personnel. But I know P.J.'s a very solid defensive coach who knows the game inside out."

Daly also pointed to another Carlesimo trait that became evident almost from the moment he took the Blazers job: P.J. is not only personable and outgoing, he's willing to mingle. Not every NBA coach has the stomach to deal with the common man, let alone

explain himself to the public. In contrast, Carlesimo hit the Portland talk-show circuit and took his chances.

"He's one of the really fun people you'll ever meet," Daly said. "It should be very, very exciting, both for P.J. and for the Portland fans."

Carlesimo freely admits he'll have to modify his coaching style if he's going to be a long-range success in the NBA—and that, more than a quick turnaround, is what Allen and his chief lieutenant, Bert Kolde, were looking for. Carlesimo was a disciplinarian at Seton Hall, which is another way of describing him as a hollerer. Shouting at NBA players as a matter of routine has gone the way of the 6-foot-7 pivot man.

Adelman was fond of saying that the NBA is a "players' league," and basically, his successor agrees with that. "I'll have to adapt the way I do some things," P.J. said, "and I know that. It's obviously a different level from college to the pros. You're going from young guys in a campus environment to men, professionals, who are making lots of money because they already have the skills and knowledge to play. A coach has to realize that, but he still has to coach, to

Jerome Kersey takes time out to chat with local Boys & Girls Club members. A $500,000 gift from the Blazers and executive suite holders in the new Rose Garden arena was instrumental in the start of construction on a 27,000 square foot club building in northeast Portland. The new facility, to be known as the Blazers Club, is the first Boys & Girls Club to be affiliated with a National Basketball Association team. The Blazers organization has long been involved in Boys & Girls Club work through visits to clubs and assistance in fund-raising projects. The Trail Blazers annually team up with numerous community service organizations throughout Oregon and southwest Washington, providing leadership in promoting the kinds of values important to the community.

BLAZERS
We
BELIEVE

Blazers refuse to die

Clyde the Glide rides high again for Blazers

New Blazers coach P.J. Carlesimo goes one-on-one with columnist Dwight Jaynes and NBA beat writer Kerry Eggers of *The Oregonian* at the June news conference announcing his appointment.

try and bring out the best in his team. That's the key at any level."

In all of these areas, with any of the current questions, the Blazers do have history on their side. Good organizations win; sloppy ones slide into mediocrity. Over a solid quarter-century, the Blazers have shown they can win through three majority owners, seven previous head coaches and countless other assistants, scouts and support staffers.

Some years it's a lot. And some it's really a lot. So even in this period of obvious transition, it would be foolish to suspect the Blazers might suddenly slump to the role of NBA doormat. Perhaps Whitsitt is right in preaching caution to Portland's excitable fans, but even if the Blazers are a bit removed from a run to the NBA Finals, there is every reason to expect they'll find their way back soon enough.

No less an authority on championships than Bill Walton believes Portland will see another dash to glory, and maybe not so far down the road. "Everything is just so solid," he said. "The Blazers will bounce up to the top again, just like they have before. And when they do, I'll be cheering for 'em as loud as anybody."

And maybe that's the real story of the Trail Blazers' 25th anniversary celebration: This is what happens when good people build a franchise the right way in just the perfect sort of city. It rolls along quite nicely, thank you, even over the bumpy spots.

A retiring athlete once was asked about his plans and he jokingly replied, "I've seen the future, and it's a lot like the present — only longer." Well, that view of things would be just fine for the proud Portland Trail Blazers, who have earned the right to salute their past, applaud the present and await the future with nothing less than unbridled enthusiasm.

Rip City is alive and well.

A LABOR OF LOVE

Sister Maxine Currin has attended only one game in the club's first quarter century, but the Newport, Oregon resident has to be ranked near the top of the list of dedicated Blazers fans. Sister Max, who grew up in the Eugene area cheering for University of Oregon teams coached by Howard Hobson, was hooked by the Trail Blazers from Day One. So hooked, in fact, that she started clipping every newspaper story about the team and its players she could find. She never missed Blazers stories on the sports pages of the state's two major dailies — *The Oregonian* and *The Oregon Journal* — and, as she moved around the state, in other newspapers she came across. Those clippings were neatly pasted into big scrapbooks with bright red covers. She started clipping stories the very first year, and by 1989-90, the team's 20th anniversary season, had amassed more than 20 of the big scrapbooks, enough to fill the back of a small pickup truck. In 1990, Sister Max gave the collection to the Blazers organization where it has become a major source for historical research including the author's preparation for writing this book. She's quick to point out that her all-time favorite basketball player is former Celtics star Larry Bird, but its obvious the Blazers also occupy a very special place in her heart. How else, then, could you explain the clipping books, which former Blazers broadcaster Pat Lafferty appropriately tagged a "true labor of love"?

C H A P T E R **8**

A SPECIAL LOOK
by George Pasero

*G*EORGE PASERO IS A LEGEND IN OREGON SPORTS JOURNALISM.
HIS 45-YEAR CAREER IN THE NEWSPAPER BUSINESS BEGAN WHEN
HE GRADUATED FROM THE UNIVERSITY OF OREGON IN 1940.
READERS THROUGHOUT THE STATE LONG ENJOYED HIS AWARD-WINNING
"PASERO SAYS" COLUMNS, WHICH APPEARED IN THE *OREGON JOURNAL* AND
THEN *THE OREGONIAN* UNTIL HIS RETIREMENT IN 1985.

NOT SO LONG AGO, THE CITY THAT SOME LOCAL PUNDITS STILL JOKING-
LY CALL STUMPTOWN WAS YEARNING MIGHTILY FOR A PROUD IDENTITY OF
ITS OWN.

STUMPTOWN, YOU ASK?

Sure, the settlers had to whack down great firs and giant alders just to be able
to drive their wagons to water. Hard to imagine looking at the Portland of
today, definitely, yet there is was: Stumptown.

But the old village was rapidly becoming a sprawling metro area that straddled
the Willamette, spread out to the bordering banks of what once was the fabled
"Mighty River of the West" — now the Columbia — and looked nigh over its
eastern shoulder to the sunrise lighting up majestic Mount Hood.

This was no longer a little Western outpost. Nor was it, as they might have
fancied in the East, someplace outside the continental shelf. Seattle, to the
north, had outpaced it in population and recognition — and that was consid-

201

erably resented by the Portland sports establishment.

It didn't help that national wire service stories still were using the dateline Portland, Oregon — to distinguish the Rose City from Portland, Maine. For historical reference, it should be noted here that a coin flip once determined that the city would be called Portland, Oregon, instead of Boston, Oregon Hey, coin flips have been tremendously influential in Portland lore. Just say Bill Walton and you get the connection, right?

More galling was that visitors always seemed to mangle the pronunciation of our area names. It's not Ore-y-GONE. Try Ore-y-gun. It's never Will-a-METTE. Always say Wil-LAM-ette. And, for what it's worth, the Willamette is this country's only major river that runs south to north.

So much for geography lessons.

The pronunciation problems continue, but at least the dateline differentiation is gone. The coming of the Portland Trail Blazers in 1970 was responsible for that. Pardon us if we point out that the NBA still hasn't expanded to Maine. At long last, the "big-league" standings carried the name of Portland, and nothing more need be added.

Growth was coming, and fast, and it would mesh with the Blazers' arrival to give Oregon a national market identity.

And yet that still didn't come easily. Later, Blazers people would talk about "Seven Years to Glory" when talking about the wonderful championship of 1977, but the reality was more like six years of trial and error that led to that magical Sunday — June 5, 1977.

'What is so rare as a day in June,' the poet James Russell Lowell asked. In Oregon, where roses bloom so profusely in June, that rarest of days brought us an NBA championship.

Rip City! Red Hot and Rollin'! Blazermania!

It was a day like none other in the annals of Portland. No, make that two rare days because the celebration kept right on going — red hot and rollin' — for another 24 hours after the Blazers dispatched the Philadelphia 76ers to win the city's first-ever big-league championship.

Sorry, David Letterman, but this was the memory that could head any list — Top 10 or otherwise. There was a crowd of 12,951 jammed into Memorial Coliseum for the historic breakthrough. But the number of people claiming to have seen the game or participated in the victory parade the next day probably could be counted in the hundreds of thousands.

You just can't find anyone who says he wasn't there.

It was a bright, sunny Sunday morning when I drove along the Willamette (pronounce it properly, please) and over the bridge toward the Coliseum for the game whose outcome would be so monumental in Portland history.

There was a calm that seemed almost eerie, with only a homeless person or two still wrapped on a blanket on the Willamette greenery. There was so little traffic. Everybody, it seemed, was sticking close to their TVs and radios. Ratings later showed that in Oregon, the game would draw a 96 percent share of the television audience — an unheard of number by any calculation.

With Walton posting his unbelievable box-score line of 20 points, 23 rebounds, 7 assists and 8 blocked shots, the Blazers were in charge most of the way. But the 76ers of Julius Erving and George McGinnis wouldn't roll over.

The Sixers closed to within two points with 16 seconds to go when McGinnis — have you heard this story before? — forced a jump ball with Bobby Gross. The 76ers gained possession and had three terrifying attempts at a basket. One was a miss, another (by Lloyd Free) was blocked by Gross and then came the final, last-gasp try by McGinnis.

Hearts were in peoples' throats from section 1 to 86, Harry Glickman said later. And that certainly included his own.

The rest is indelible.

Walton partially controlled the rebound, whirled and tapped the ball out to Johnny Davis, who bolted away from the basket and down the floor. The clock finally ran out and Johnny threw the ball wildly toward the ceiling in jubilation.

Within seconds, Walton ripped off his jersey and threw it into the stands. Fans were going berserk. Blazermania took over, but it was all joyful, nothing untoward.

The celebration spilled over into the streets with impromptu parades and dances. Thousands of posters and T-shirts popped up: "Rip City," naturally. "We're No. 1!" And of course, "Red Hot and Rollin." Fans milled around, just wanting to mingle and hug and be a part of it, cherishing this wonderful moment with everyone around them.

Glickman would later write in his autobiography: "In the *Washington Star*, a sports writer wrote: 'It was like Washington when the Senators won the World Series in 1924 or Brooklyn when the Dodgers reached "next year" in 1955 or the entire U.S. on V-J Day.' "

These are the bulldozer and backhoe operators, the truck drivers, operating engineers, carpenters, electricians, plumbers, metal workers, safety and traffic guards—men and women from every construction trade who are building the Portland Trail Blazers' new home, the $262 million Rose Garden complex adjacent to Memorial Coliseum.

During the summer of 1993, a new group of Trail Blazers came into focus. While these men and women arrived on the scene late in the first 25 years of the team's history, their efforts will have enormous impact on the organization, the City of Portland and the entire State of Oregon for decades beyond.

On the first page of this section is a rendering by Art Zendarski Architectural Illustration of San Francisco showing what the Rose Garden and the surrounding area will look like when completed in the summer of 1995. When finished the new campus, dubbed the Rose Quarter, will include a 20,000-plus seat arena, a new building called One Center Court with restaurants and offices, three parking structures, a refurbished Memorial Coliseum, and the city's largest pedestrian plaza, Portland Commons.

They dig the holes, drive the stakes, guide giant cranes, pour cement, tie re-bar, climb towers, use jack-hammers, install wiring, read plans, eye surveying stakes. They haul, measure, trim, smooth, sand, pound, drill, weld, cut and fit. They endure noise, rain, mud, dust, cold and heat.

So, it is entirely fitting that space in a book celebrating the team's 25th anniversary be dedicated to those who are building for the Blazers' and Portland's future. Photographer Michael Mather has beautifully recorded the construction progress on the new arena and adjacent structures through the men and women on the job. Unfortunately, these pages can give only a small sampling of all those who are involved.

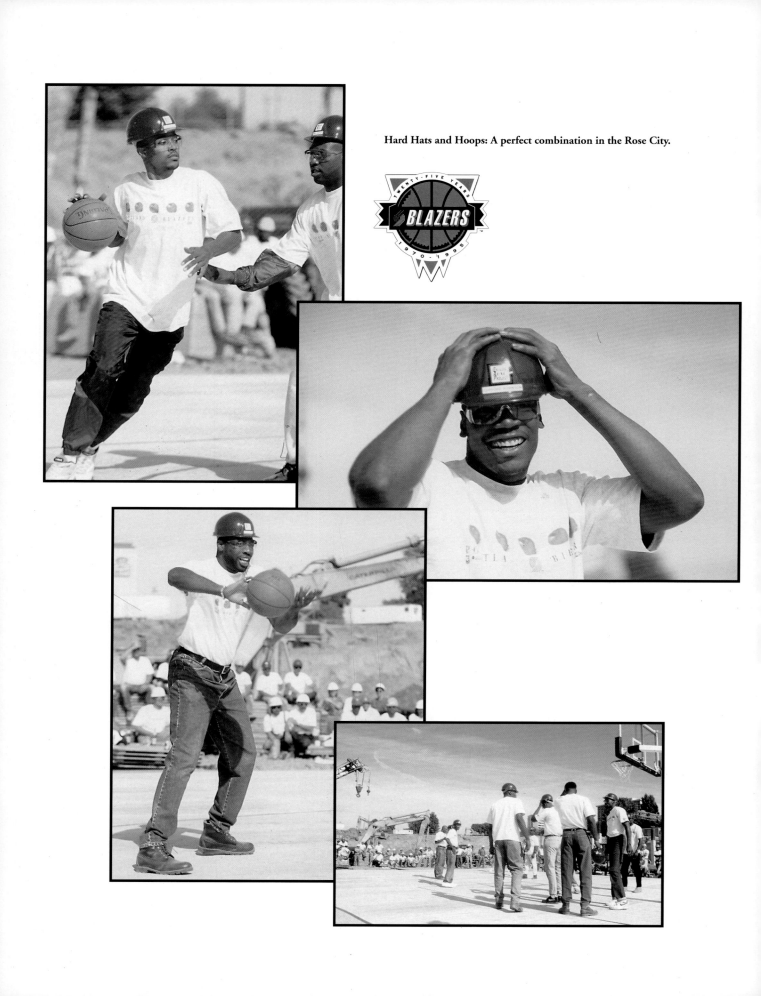

Hard Hats and Hoops: A perfect combination in the Rose City.

George gives Mychal Thompson a hi-five as he leaves the floor.

So that reporter was just a little outrageous with his comparisons. Who cared?

Some of the best, most hilarious episodes were still to come. The next day, Monday, the city put together a hastily arranged parade. Wasn't that what all true champions did?

It was a morning bursting with euphoria. The Blazermaniacs just kept coming, packing downtown with what was later estimated as 250,000 people. The parade started at the foot of Broadway with the players and their wives, and the coaches and their wives, riding in convertibles to Terry Schrunk Plaza near City Hall. It was estimated that the parade would last about an hour. Well, it took almost three hours to navigate the 12 blocks. Twelve blocks of sidewalk-to-sidewalk people, you could say.

Walton and his wife Susan, who did things their own way, arrived at the assembly point on their bicycles. They had no chance after that. It was ride or be mobbed. The bikes were parked and the city's most renowned redhead bobbed along in an open convertible. Later, a report circulated that Bill's bike had been stolen. Not quite. It turned out that someone decided to protect it — and returned the bicycle undamaged.

My favorite memory of the ceremony at Schrunk Plaza was that of Walton holding a bottle of beer over the head of Portland Mayor Neil Goldschmidt and, laughing all the time, spilling it down His Honor's neck. Neil, a former basketball player, was a Blazers fan like everyone else, so he merely grimaced and shook his head.

This was a city that finally came to fully appreciate Walton the ballplayer, even if some citizens weren't quite ready to make peace with the young rebel and his background of anti-government resentment. The term "politically correct" wasn't in vogue at that time, but if it had been, it would have been used to describe what Walton was not.

In Portland, as Walton himself would say much later, a "shy and immature" young man did not always adhere to the mores of those in his new locale.

TV sportscaster Doug LaMear got a lot of attention one night when he suggested — prior to the '77 championship, of course — that Portland "...ought to trade Walton for a six-pack of carrot juice."

Say this, though: No one played the game with more gusto — enjoyment, if you will — and all-around talent than Walton. And in the championship season, after two years fighting off injuries, he was as healthy as he ever would be again. Walton's supporting cast was immensely talented, too, but Bill was the on-court sparkplug, the leader, the no-nonsense warrior when it came to playing the game the right way — and that had a lot to do with the way of Coach Jack Ramsay.

What a match. Neither could have been more fortunate, and once that NBA title was in their hands, Oregonians by the thousands ignored Walton's previous injuries, his politics, his dietary preferences, his occasional intemperate statements and everything else to celebrate a wondrous year of basketball triumph with him — and with all the Blazers.

The following season, the nation's fans eventually came to be in awe of a team which seemed to be playing the game as well as it ever had been done. This was the Blazers team that was 50-10 when Walton and then others were injured. With Walton limping and then forced to the sidelines, they were eliminated in the first round of the playoffs by Seattle.

The joy of 1977 would sadly prove so ephemeral. So long, dynasty.

Regardless, the level of Blazers basketball had been elevated to playoff level and the team has pretty much breathed that same rarified air ever since. They've missed postseason play just once since 1977.

Blazermania remains, albeit somewhat muffled at times — such as when the club "struggled" to a 47-win regular season in 1993-94. Still, the sellouts continue, game after game, at a pace that far outstrips anything pro sports has ever known.

On the victory stand while he waited for the parade

to reach him on that glorious June 6, 1977, Harry Glickman could recall how he'd pursued his dream of bringing his hometown into the major leagues. In the midst of that happy reverie, Harry gave way to his emotions and spoke of his mother, who was in a home for aged but had become very much a Blazers fan. He talked of his family, of two of the club's owners — Herman Sarkowsky and Larry Weinberg — who'd taken a risk and kept the faith, and of two old friends who had been with him since Day One, George Rickles and Beryln Hodges. And women, too: Sandy Sedillo, Gail Miller, Mary Conchuratt and Meredith Wayt.

Remember, the Blazers were a franchise that had to be built from scratch. It was hardly easy going in the early days, but all these faithful, hard-working people had stuck it out. They were rewarded with a championship in 1977, but also they had laid the foundation for something much larger — a franchise that now ranks among the very proudest in professional sports.

It's worth recalling that the Blazers were not an instant success, certainly not in the won-lost column but also in the battle to win fans' hearts. Portlanders didn't exactly beat down the door of Memorial Coliseum to see the new kids on the sports block. Big-league label or not, the Blazers had to win over the skeptics. Portland's first league game drew only 4,273 — well under the average for Glickman's popular ice hockey team, the Portland Buckaroos.

Understand that Oregonians were experiencing considerable ambivalence. The sports-minded were yearning for major-league exposure, but the majority wanted

George Pasero

to protect their environment and treasured livability. The state's governor, Tom McCall, was busy saving the beaches and river greenways for future generations. McCall even once gave this advice to tourists: "Visit, but don't stay."

For the record, though, McCall was right there, front and center, for opening night in the NBA — proving, perhaps, that you could champion the saving of beaches and forests and still come to appreciate the value of the state's first major-league team.

History has shown, pretty obviously, that Oregonians can enjoy the wonderful living this great state provides, and yet go truly bonkers over an NBA team that has given them countless thrills over the years — and which has become such a solid rock in the community itself.

No story of mine regarding the Blazers and their impact on Oregon — in fact, no story of mine in 50 years of writing sports — would be complete without my own reflection on Harry Glickman. Not to mention my admiration, my friendship, my affection for him over all these years. I was there for all his great successes and, yes, for a few failures, too. Hey, who's infallible?

Harry represents the great American success story.

He grew up in Old South Portland in what was then a Jewish/Italian neighborhood. He sold papers at age eight, while his mother supported her only child by working as a garment finisher in the women's clothing industry.

"I never went hungry," Harry said, and he went on to play various sports, including basketball, at Lincoln High.

It was a long time later, but Harry's work ethic, his

ambition and his doggedness led to the fulfillment of a dream when he brought this major-league basketball team to Portland.

Harry had been pursuing an NBA team for 15 years before it actually became reality. In the 1950s, he did very well promoting one or two NFL exhibition games per year in Portland — meanwhile promoting whatever else he could in between.

By 1954, he was carrying on a voluminous but unsuccessful correspondence with then-NBA commissioner Maurice Podoloff. Then in 1957-58, Harry actually brought an NBA preseason game to the area, and lured the Boston Celtics, besides. Never mind that the Coliseum hadn't yet been completed. Harry took the game across the river to Vancouver and drew 3,800 in a gym that didn't really seat that many. By '59, he'd pulled an NBA regular-season game to town, and staged it in the Multnomah County livestock arena.

Fortunately for all concerned, the Coliseum was coming. It had been approved after a crucial 1954 campaign that might have turned when *Oregon Journal* editorial writer Tom Humphrey challenged the citizenry with this ringing headline: "Big League City or Sad Sack Town?"

Voters responded by approving a package that not only provided for the Coliseum — their very own Glass Palace — but also a new bridge over the Willamette and improved street lighting. Portland was coming out of the dark in more ways than one.

Glickman brought the Western Hockey League Buckaroos in as the Coliseum's first full-time tenant, and they were a smash, drawing good crowds and fin-

ishing first nine times in 13 years. Harry had finally gotten on a roll that wouldn't stop until he'd landed an NBA expansion team and then seen it blossom into a champion.

In 1993, when Harry was chosen Portland's First Citizen, longtime area newspaperman Wayne Thompson wrote: "This homegrown entrepreneur accomplished something other notable Oregonians did not achieve in their fruitful lifetimes — he gave Oregon a national market identity. He delivered the enterprise that gave city and state an identity that helped spur growth in all economic sectors.

"It is difficult to quantify the economic impact of Glickman's Trail Blazers. Exposing the Portland area to national TV audiences can't be measured in direct dollar terms. In 1992 alone, though, the Blazers generated millions of dollars in convention business when, in a two-month span, the organization was host to the NBA championship finals, the NBA draft and the pre-Olympic basketball tournament featuring the first 'Dream Team.' "

More than that, though, Harry Glickman has been a Portland loyalist forever and a man who gives back to his community in so many worthy endeavors.

Harry's great dream of top-level sports for his city became reality with the coming of the Blazers. But imagine where we will be headed in 1995 when owner Paul Allen and city officials join Harry for the opening of an incredible, $262 million Rose Garden arena complex.

Go, Blazers — and thanks, Harry, for charting the way toward a great new century.

Memories

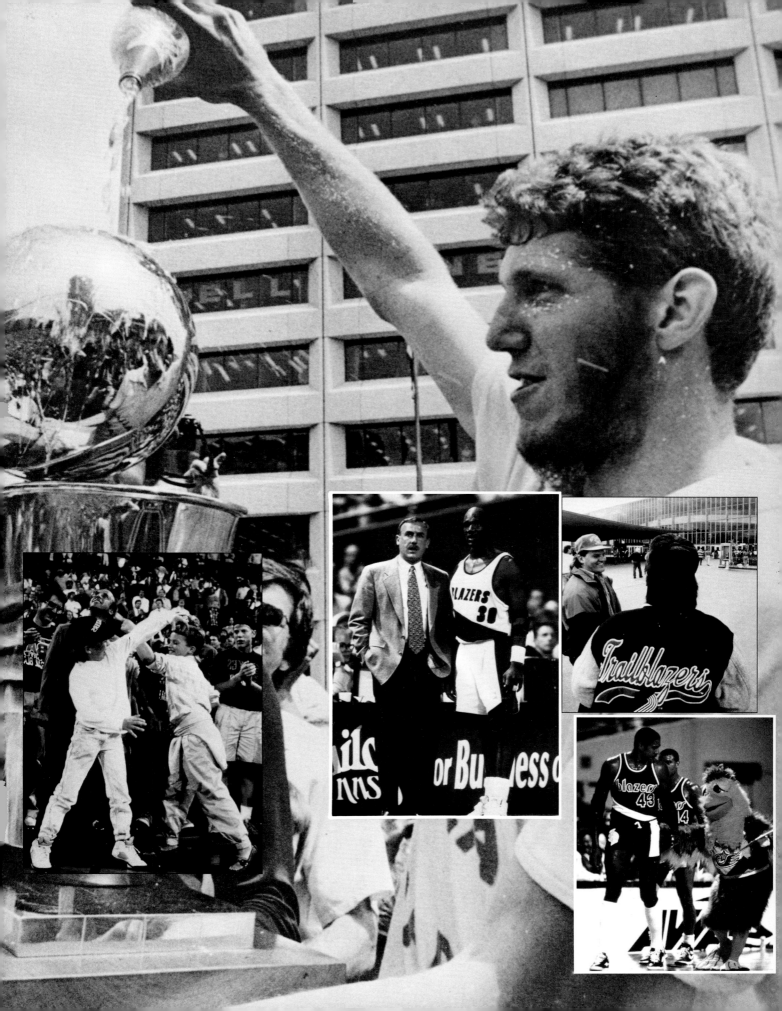

CHAPTER 10

Stats & Records

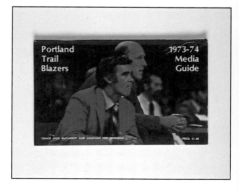

ALL TIME PORTLAND TRAIL BLAZERS ROSTER

INCLUDES ALL 150 PLAYERS WHO HAVE APPEARED IN ONE OR MORE NBA REGULAR
SEASON GAMES AS A TRAIL BLAZER
*ORIGINAL TRAIL BLAZER (ON ROSTER FOR FIRST GAME)

A

Abdelnaby, Alaa (F), Duke	1990-92
Adelman, Rick (G), Loyola-Marymount	1970-73*
Ainge, Danny (G), Brigham Young	1990-92
Anderson, Danny (G), USC	1974-76
Anderson, Kim (F), Missouri	1978-79
Anderson, Richard (F), UC-Santa Barbara	1987-89
Awtrey, Dennis (C), Santa Clara	1981-82

B

Bailey, Carl (C), Tuskegee	1981-82
Barnett, Jim (F), Oregon	1970-71*
Bates, Billy Ray (G), Kentucky State	1979-82
Berry, Walter (F), St. John's	1986-87
Binion, Joe (F), North Carolina A&T	1986-87
Bowie, Sam (C), Kentucky	1984-89
Branch, Adrian (F), Maryland	1988-89
Brewer, Jim (F), Minnesota	1979-80
Brewer, Ron (G), Arkansas	1978-81
Bryant, Mark (F), Seton Hall	1988-
Buse, Don (G), Evansville	1982-83

C

Calhoun, Corky (F), Pennsylvania	1976-78
Carr, Kenny (F), North Carolina State	1982-87
Clemens, Barry (F), Ohio Wesleyan	1974-76
Colter, Steve (G), New Mexico State	1984-86
Cooper, Wayne (C), New Orleans	1982-84, 89-92
Crompton Geoff (C), North Carolina	1980-81

D

Davis, Bob (F), Weber State	1972-73
Davis, Charlie (G), Wake Forest	1972-74
Davis, Johnny (G), Dayton	1976-78
Davis, Walter (F), North Carolina	1990-91
Dischinger, Terry (F), Purdue	1972-73
Dorsey, Jacky (F), Georgia	1977-78
Drexler, Clyde (G), Houston	1983-
Dudley, Chris (C), Yale	1993-
Duckworth, Kevin (C), Eastern Illinois	1986-93
Dunn, T.R. (G), Alabama	1977-80

E

Elie, Mario (G), American International	1992-93
Ellis, LeRoy (C), St. John's	1970-71*
Engler, Chris (C), Wyoming	1986-87
English, Claude (G), Rhode Island	1970-71*

F

Ferreira, Rolando (C), Houston	1988-89
Fryer, Bernie (G), Brigham Young	1973-74

G

Gale, Mike (G), Elizabeth City State	1980-81
Gamble, Kevin (G), Iowa	1987-88
Gilliam, Herm (G), Purdue	1976-77
Gilmore, Walt (F), Fort Valley State	1970-71*
Grant, Harvey (F), Oklahoma	1993-
Gregor, Gary (F), South Carolina	1970-72*
Gross, Bob (F), Long Beach State	1975-82
Gudmundsson, Petur (C), Washington	1981-82

H

Halimon, Shaler (F), Utah State	1970-71
Hamilton, Roy (G), UCLA	1980-81
Harper, Michael (F), North Park	1980-82
Hawes, Steve (C), Washington	1975-76
Hollins, Lionel (G), Arizona State	1975-80
Holton, Michael (G), UCLA	1986-88

I

Imhoff, Darrall (C), California	1971-72
Irvin, Byron (G), Missouri	1989-90

J

Jackson, Jaren (G), Georgetown	1993-
Jeelani, Abdul (F), Wisconsin-Parkside	1979-80
Johnson, Clemon (C), Florida A&M	1978-79
Johnson, Dave (G), Syracuse	1992-93
Johnson, John (F), Iowa	1973-76
Johnson, Ken (F), Michigan State	1985-86
Johnson, Ollie (F), Temple	1972-74
Johnson, Steve (C), Oregon State	1986-89
Johnston, Nate (F), Tampa	1989-90
Jones, Caldwell (C), Albany State	1985-89
Jones, Charles (F), Louisville	1987-88
Jones, Robin (C), St. Louis	1976-77
Jones, Steve (G), Oregon	1975-76
Jordan, Ed (G), Rutgers	1983-84
Judkins, Jeff (F), Utah	1982-83

K

Kersey, Jerome (F), Longwood	1984-
Knight, Ron (F), Los Angeles State	1970-72*
Kunnert, Kevin (C), Iowa	1979-82

L

Lamp, Jeff (F), Virginia	1981-84
Layton, Dennis (G), USC	1973-74
Lee, Greg (G), UCLA	1975-76
Lever, Lafayette (G), Arizona State	1982-84
Lucas, Maurice (F), Marquette	1976-80, 87-88
Lumpkin, Phil (G), Miami-Ohio	1974-75

M

Manning, Ed (F), Jackson State	1970-71*
Marsh, Jim (F), USC	1971-72
Martin, Brian (F), Kansas	1985-86
Martin, Fernando (F), Club Real Madrid	1986-87
Martin, LaRue (C), Loyola-Chicago	1972-76
Mayes, Clyde (F), Furman	1976-77
McCarter, Willie (G), Drake	1971-72
McDowell, Hank (F), Memphis State	1982-83
McKenzie, Stan (G), New York U.	1970-73*
McMillian, Jim (G), Columbia	1978-79
Murphy, Ronnie (G), Jacksonville	1987-88
Murray, Tracy (F), UCLA	1992-
Murrey, Dorie (F), Detroit	1970-71*

N

Natt, Calvin (F), NE Louisiana	1979-84
Neal, Craig (G), Georgia Tech	1988-89
Neal, Lloyd (F), Tennessee State	1972-79
Norris, Audie (F), Jackson State	1982-85
Norwood, Willie (F), Alcorn A&M	1977-78

O

Owens, Tom (C), South Carolina	1977-81

P

Pack, Robert (G), USC	1991-92
Paxson, Jim (G), Dayton	1979-88
Petrie, Geoff (G), Princeton	1970-76*
Petrovic, Drazen (G), Cibona Zagreb	1989-91
Piotrowski, Tom (C), LaSalle	1983-84
Porter, Terry (G), Wisconsin-Stevens Point	1985-

R

Ransey, Kelvin (G), Ohio State	1980-82
Reid, Robert (F), St. Mary's-Texas	1989-90
Roberson, Rick (C), Cincinnati	1973-74
Robinson, Clifford (F), Connecticut	1989-
Robinson, James (G), Alabama	1993-
Rowan, Ron (G), St. John's	1986-87
Rudd, Delaney (G), Wake Forest	1992-93

S

Scheffler, Tom (C), Purdue	1984-85
Schlueter, Dale (C), Colorado State	1970-72, 77-78*
Sibley, Mark (G), Northwestern	1973-74

Sichting, Jerry (G), Purdue	1987-89
Smith, Bill (C), Syracuse	1971-73
Smith, Greg (F), Western Kentucky	1972-76
Smith, Reggie (C), Texas Christian	1992-
Smith, Willie (G), Missouri	1978-79
Steele, Larry (G), Kentucky	1971-80
Steppe, Brook (F), Georgia Tech	1988-89
Stricker, Bill (F), U. of Pacific	1970-71
Strickland, Rod (G), DePaul	1992-
Strothers, Lamont (G), College of Newport	1991-92

T

Terrell, Ira (F), Southern Methodist	1978-79
Thompson, Bernard (G), Fresno State	1984-85
Thompson, Kevin (C), North Carolina St.	1993-
Thompson, Mychal (C), Minnesota	1978-86
Townes, Linton (F), James Madison	1982-83
Turner, Bill (F), Akron	1972-73
Twardzik, Dave (G), Old Dominion	1976-80

V

Valentine, Darnell (G), Kansas	1981-86
Vandeweghe, Kiki (F), UCLA	1984-89
Verga, Bob (G), Duke	1973-74
Verhoeven, Peter (F), Fresno State	1981-84

W

Walker, Wally (F), Virginia	1976-78
Walton, Bill (C), UCLA	1974-78
Washington, Kermit (F), American U.	1979-82
Whatley, Ennis (G), Alabama	1991-92
Wheeler, Clinton (G), Wm. Patterson	1988-89
Wicks, Sidney (F), UCLA	1971-76
Wilkens, Lenny (G), Providence	1974-75
Williams, Buck (F), Maryland	1989-
Wilson, Nikita (F), Louisiana State	1987-88
Wohl, Dave (G), Pennsylvania	1972-73
Wolf, Joe (F), North Carolina	1992-93

Y

Yelverton, Charles (G), Fordham	1971-72
Young, Danny (G), Wake Forest	1988-92
Young, Perry (G), Virginia Tech	1986-87

1970-71 (29-53)
Coach: Rolland Todd

Adelman*	Knight*
Barnett*	Manning
Ellis*	McKenzie
English	Murrey
Gilmore	Petrie*
Gregor	Schlueter
Halimon	Stricker

1971-72 (18-64)
Coaches: Rolland Todd
Stu Inman

Adelman*	Schlueter*
Gregor*	B. Smith
Imhoff	Steele
Knight	Petrie
Marsh	Wicks*
McCarter*	Yelverton
McKenzie	

1972-73 (21-61)
Coach: Jack McCloskey
Assistant: Neil Johnston

Adelman*	Petrie*
B. Davis	B. Smith
C. Davis	G. Smith
Dischinger*	Steele
O. Johnson	Turner
L. Martin	Wicks*
McKenzie	Wohl
L. Neal*	

1973-74 (27-55)
Coach: Jack McCloskey
Assistant: Neil Johnston

C. Davis	Petrie*
Fryer	Roberson*
J. Johnson*	Sibley
O. Johnson*	G. Smith
Layton	Steele*
L. Martin	Verga
L. Neal	Wicks

1974-75 (38-44)
Coach: Lenny Wilkens
Assistant: Tom Meschery

D. Anderson	Petrie*
Clemens	G. Smith
J. Johnson*	Steele
Lumpkin	Walton*
L. Martin	Wicks*
L. Neal	Wilkens*

1975-76 (37-45)
Coach: Lenny Wilkens
Assistant: Tom Meschery

D. Anderson	L. Martin
Clemens	L. Neal*
Gross	Petrie*
Hawes	G. Smith
Hollins	Steele*
J. Johnson	Walton*
S. Jones	Wicks*
Lee	

1976-77 (49-33)
Jack Ramsay
Assistant: Jack McKinney

Calhoun	Mayes
J. Davis	L. Neal
Gilliam	Steele
Gross*	Twardzik*
Hollins*	Walker
R. Jones	Walton*
Lucas*	

1977-78 (58-24)
Coach: Jack Ramsay
Assistant: Jack McKinney

Calhoun	Norwood
J. Davis	Owens
Dorsey	Schlueter
Dunn	Steele
Gross*	Twardzik*
Hollins*	Walker
Lucas*	Walton*
L. Neal	

1978-79 (45-37)
Coach: Jack Ramsay
Assistant: Jack McKinney

K. Anderson	L. Neal
R. Brewer	Owens*
Dunn*	W. Smith
Gross	Steele
Hollins*	Terrell
C. Johnson	M. Thompson*
Lucas	Twardzik*
McMillian	

1979-80 (38-44)
Coach: Jack Ramsay
Assistant: Bucky Buckwalter

Bates	Lucas
J. Brewer	Natt
R. Brewer*	Owens*
Dunn	Paxson
Gross	Steele*
Hollins*	Twardzik
Jeelani	Washington*
Kunnert	

1980-81 (45-37)
Coach: Jack Ramsay
Assistant: Bucky Buckwalter

Bates	Kunnert
R. Brewer*	Natt*
Crompton	Owens*
Gale	Paxson*
Gross	Ransey
Hamilton	Thompson
Harper	Washington*

1981-82 (42-40)
Coach: Jack Ramsay
Assistants: Jimmy Lynam, Bucky Buckwalter

Awtrey	Natt*
Bailey	Paxson*
Bates	Ransey*
Gross	M. Thompson*
Gudmundsson	Valentine
Harper*	Verhoeven
Kunnert	Washington
Lamp	

1982-83 (46-36)
Coach: Jack Ramsay
Assistants: Jimmy Lynam, Bucky Buckwalter

Buse	Natt*
Carr*	Norris
Cooper	Paxson*
Judkins	M. Thompson*
Lamp	Townes
Lever	Valentine*
McDowell	Verhoeven

1983-84 (48-34)
Coach: Jack Ramsay
Assistants: Rick Adelman, Bucky Buckwalter

Carr	Norris
Cooper*	Paxson*
Drexler	Piotrowski
Jordan	M. Thompson*
Lamp	Valentine*
Lever	Verhoeven
Natt*	

1984-85 (42-40)
Coach: Jack Ramsay
Assistants: Rick Adelman, Bucky Buckwalter

Bowie	Paxson*
Carr	Scheffler
Colter	B. Thompson
Drexler*	M. Thompson*
Kersey	Valentine*
Norris	Vandeweghe*

1985-86 (40-42)
Coach: Jack Ramsay
Assistants: Rick Adelman, Bucky Buckwalter

Bowie*	B. Martin
Carr	Paxson
Colter	Porter
Drexler*	M. Thompson*
K. Johnson	Valentine*
Ca. Jones	Vandeweghe*
Kersey	

1986-87 (49-33)
Coach: Mike Schuler
Assistants: Rick Adelman, Jack Schalow

Berry	Ca. Jones
Binion	Kersey
Bowie*	F. Martin
Carr*	Paxson
Drexler*	Porter*
Duckworth	Rowan
Engler	Vandeweghe*
Holton	P. Young
S. Johnson	

1987-88 (53-29)
Coach: Mike Schuler
Assistants: Rick Adelman, Jack Schalow

R. Anderson	Kersey
Drexler*	Lucas
Duckworth	Murphy
Gamble	Paxson
Holton	Porter*
S. Johnson*	Sichting
Ca. Jones*	Vandeweghe*
Ch. Jones	Wilson

1988-89 (39-43)
Coaches: Mike Schuler
Rick Adelman
Assistants: Rick Adelman, Jack Schalow,
John Wetzel, Maurice Lucas

R. Anderson	Kersey*
Bowie	C. Neal
Branch	Porter*
Bryant*	Sichting
Drexler*	Steppe
Duckworth*	Vandeweghe
Ferreira	Wheeler
S. Johnson	D. Young
Ca. Jones	

1989-90 (59-23)
Coach: Rick Adelman
Assistants: Jack Schalow, John Wetzel

Bryant	Petrovic
Cooper	Porter*
Drexler*	Reid
Duckworth*	C. Robinson
Irvin	Williams*
Johnston	D. Young
Kersey*	

1990-91 (63-19)
Coach: Rick Adelman
Assistants: Jack Schalow, John Wetzel

Abdelnaby	Kersey*
Ainge	Petrovic
Bryant	Porter*
Cooper	C. Robinson
W. Davis	Williams*
Drexler*	D. Young
Duckworth*	

1991-92 (57-25)
Coach: Rick Adelman
Assistants: Jack Schalow, John Wetzel

Abdelnaby	Pack
Ainge	Porter*
Bryant	C. Robinson
Cooper	Strothers
Drexler*	Whatley
Duckworth*	Williams*
Kersey*	D. Young

1992-93 (51-31)
Coach: Rick Adelman
Assistants: Jack Schalow, John Wetzel

Bryant	Porter*
Drexler*	C. Robinson
Duckworth*	Rudd
Elie	R. Smith
D. Johnson	Strickland
Kersey*	Williams*
Murray	Wolf*

1993-94 (47-35)
Coach: Rick Adelman
Assistants: Jack Schalow, John Wetzel, Kip Motta

Bryant	Porter*
Drexler*	C. Robinson
Dudley*	J. Robinson
Grant	R. Smith
Jackson	Strickland
Kersey*	K. Thompson
Murray	Williams*

		REGULAR SEASON			PLAYOFFS		
Year	Coach	W	L	Pct.	W	L	Pct.
1970-71	Rolland Todd	29	53	.354	—	—	—
1971-72	Rolland Todd	12	44	.214			
	Stu Inman	6	20	.231	—	—	—
1972-73	Jack McCloskey	21	61	.256	—	—	—
1973-74	Jack McCloskey	27	55	.329	—	—	—
1974-75	Lenny Wilkens	38	44	.463	—	—	—
1975-76	Lenny Wilkens	37	45	.451	—	—	—
1976-77	Jack Ramsay	49	33	.598	14	5	.737
1977-78	Jack Ramsay	58	24	.707	2	4	.333
1978-79	Jack Ramsay	45	37	.549	1	2	.333
1979-80	Jack Ramsay	38	44	.463	1	2	.333
1980-81	Jack Ramsay	45	37	.549	1	2	.333
1981-82	Jack Ramsay	42	40	.512	—	—	—
1982-83	Jack Ramsay	46	36	.561	3	4	.429
1983-84	Jack Ramsay	48	34	.585	2	3	.400
1984-85	Jack Ramsay	42	40	.512	4	5	.444
1985-86	Jack Ramsay	40	42	.488	1	3	.250
1986-87	Mike Schuler	49	33	.598	1	3	.250
1987-88	Mike Schuler	53	29	.646	1	3	.250
1988-89	Mike Schuler	25	22	.532			
	Rick Adelman	14	21	.400	0	3	.000
1989-90	Rick Adelman	59	23	.720	12	9	.571
1990-91	Rick Adelman	63	19	.768	9	7	.563
1991-92	Rick Adelman	57	25	.695	13	8	.619
1992-93	Rick Adelman	51	31	.622	1	3	.250
1993-94	Rick Adelman	47	35	.538	1	3	.250
Totals		1041	927	.529	67	69	.493

BLAZERS COACHING RECORDS

		REGULAR SEASON				PLAYOFFS		
	Years	G	W	L	Pct.	G	W	L	Pct.
Rolland Todd	2+	138	41	97	.297	—	—	—	—
Stu Inman	1	26	6	20	.231	—	—	—	—
Jack McCloskey	2	164	48	116	.293	—	—	—	—
Lenny Wilkens	2	164	75	89	.457	—	—	—	—
Jack Ramsay	10	820	453	367	.552	59	29	30	.492
Mike Schuler	2+	211	127	84	.602	8	2	6	.250
Rick Adelman	5+	445	291	154	.654	69	36	33	.522
Totals	24	1968	1041	927	.529	136	67	69	.493

ALL-TIME TRAIL BLAZERS CAREER LEADERS

THROUGH 1993-94 SEASON

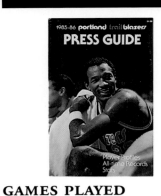

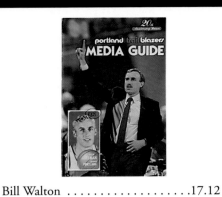

GAMES PLAYED

Clyde Drexler	.826
Jerome Kersey	.768
Terry Porter	.723
Jim Paxson	.627
Larry Steele	.610
Mychal Thompson	.551
Kevin Duckworth	.527
Bob Gross	.486
Geoff Petrie	.446
Lloyd Neal	.435

MINUTES PLAYED

Clyde Drexler	.28,098
Terry Porter	.23,208
Jerome Kersey	.20,257
Mychal Thompson	.18,913
Jim Paxson	.18,398
Geoff Petrie	.16,787
Sidney Wicks	.15,456
Larry Steele	.14,777
Kevin Duckworth	.14,595
Buck Williams	.13,036

POINTS

Clyde Drexler	.17,136
Terry Porter	.11,018
Jim Paxson	.10,003
Geoff Petrie	.9,732
Jerome Kersey	.9,559
Mychal Thompson	.9,215
Sidney Wicks	.8,882
Kevin Duckworth	.7,188
Kiki Vandeweghe	.6,698
Clifford Robinson	.5,936

SCORING AVERAGE

(Minimum 100 games)

Kiki Vandeweghe	.23.50
Sidney Wicks	.22.32
Geoff Petrie	.21.82
Clyde Drexler	.20.75
Calvin Natt	.17.23

Bill Walton	.17.12
Mychal Thompson	.16.72
John Johnson	.15.99
Jim Paxson	.15.95
Kelvin Ransey	.15.63

FIELD GOALS MADE

Clyde Drexler	.6,584
Jim Paxson	.4,058
Geoff Petrie	.3,970
Terry Porter	.3,896
Jerome Kersey	.3,778
Mychal Thompson	.3,777
Sidney Wicks	.3,502
Kevin Duckworth	.2,848
Kiki Vandeweghe	.2,531
Clifford Robinson	.2,342

FGS ATTEMPTED

Clyde Drexler	.13,713
Geoff Petrie	.8,719
Terry Porter	.8,239
Jim Paxson	.8,075
Jerome Kersey	.7,872
Sidney Wicks	.7,605
Mychal Thompson	.7,476
Kevin Duckworth	.6,000
Clifford Robinson	.5,151
Kiki Vandeweghe	.4,809

FIELD GOAL PCT.

(Minimum 1,000 made)

Buck Williams	..564
Calvin Natt	..545
Steve Johnson	..540
Kiki Vandeweghe	..526
Kenny Carr	..524
Tom Owens	..520
Bob Gross	..514
Bill Walton	..510
Mychal Thompson	..505
Jim Paxson	..503

3-PT. FIELD GOALS MADE

Terry Porter	.729
Clyde Drexler	.377
Danny Ainge	.180
Richard Anderson	.91
Kiki Vandeweghe	.89
Jim Paxson	.87
Danny Young	.72
Tracy Murray	.71
Steve Colter	.53
Clifford Robinson	.51

3-PT. FIELD GOALS ATT.

Terry Porter	.1,892
Clyde Drexler	.1,291
Danny Ainge	.481
Jim Paxson	.378
Richard Anderson	.276
Danny Young	.222
Kiki Vandeweghe	.218
Clifford Robinson	.204
Tracy Murray	.179
Steve Colter	.157

3-PT. FIELD GOAL PCT.

(Minimum 30 made)

Drazen Petrovic	..438
Kiki Vandeweghe	..408
Tracy Murray	..397
Terry Porter	..385
Danny Ainge	..374
Mario Elie	..349
Steve Colter	..338
Richard Anderson	..330
Danny Young	..323
Clyde Drexler	..292

FREE THROWS MADE

Clyde Drexler	.3,591
Terry Porter	.2,497
Jerome Kersey	.1,976
Sidney Wicks	.1,878
Jim Paxson	.1,800

Geoff Petrie 1,792	
Mychal Thompson 1,661	
Kiki Vandeweghe 1,547	
Kevin Duckworth 1,492	
Calvin Natt 1,215	

FREE THROWS ATTEMPTED
Clyde Drexler 4,568
Terry Porter 2,938
Jerome Kersey 2,839
Sidney Wicks 2,634
Mychal Thompson 2,596
Jim Paxson 2,239
Geoff Petrie 2,225
Kevin Duckworth 2,001
Clifford Robinson 1,771
Kiki Vandeweghe 1,755

FREE THROW PCT.
(Minimum 500 made)
Kiki Vandeweghe 881
Terry Porter 850
Stan McKenzie 834
Dave Twardzik 823
Geoff Petrie 805
Jim Paxson 804
Bob Gross 802
Larry Steele 796
Clyde Drexler 786
Darnell Valentine 778

TOTAL REBOUNDS
Clyde Drexler 5,105
Mychal Thompson 4,878
Jerome Kersey 4,822
Sidney Wicks 4,086
Buck Williams 3,788
Lloyd Neal 3,370
Kevin Duckworth 3,327
Maurice Lucas 2,876
Bill Walton 2,822
Kenny Carr 2,545

REBOUNDING AVERAGE
(Minimum 100 games)
Bill Walton 13.50
Sidney Wicks 10.27
Kermit Washington 9.51
Buck Williams 9.35
Mychal Thompson 8.85
Dale Schlueter 8.83
Maurice Lucas 8.72
Sam Bowie 8.07
Kenny Carr 8.05
Lloyd Neal 7.75

OFFENSIVE REBOUNDS
Clyde Drexler 2,143
Jerome Kersey 1,807
Mychal Thompson 1,489
Buck Williams 1,284
Kevin Duckworth 1,163
Bob Gross 908
Maurice Lucas 835
Tom Owens 812
Calvin Natt 799
Kenny Carr 757

DEFENSIVE REBOUNDS
Mychal Thompson 3,389
Jerome Kersey 3,015
Clyde Drexler 2,962
Buck Williams 2,504
Bill Walton 2,269
Kevin Duckworth 2,164
Maurice Lucas 2,041
Terry Porter 2,019
Kenny Carr 1,788
Lloyd Neal 1,717

ASSISTS
Terry Porter 5,186
Clyde Drexler 4,725
Geoff Petrie 2,057
Jim Paxson 2,007
Mychal Thompson 1,848
Larry Steele 1,719
Jerome Kersey 1,680
Sidney Wicks 1,647
Darnell Valentine 1,619
Bob Gross 1,447

ASSISTS AVERAGE
(Minimum 100 games)
Rod Strickland 8.12
Terry Porter 7.17
Kelvin Ransey 7.03
Clyde Drexler 5.71
Darnell Valentine 5.40
Lafayette Lever 4.92
Geoff Petrie 4.61
Rick Adelman 4.59
Bill Walton 4.42
Lionel Hollins 4.36

STEALS
Clyde Drexler 1,721
Terry Porter 1,152
Jerome Kersey 1,007
Jim Paxson 857
Larry Steele 846
Lionel Hollins 598
Bob Gross 593
Mychal Thompson 504

Darnell Valentine 494
Clifford Robinson 432

BLOCKED SHOTS
Mychal Thompson 768
Jerome Kersey 587
Clyde Drexler 572
Bill Walton 533
Clifford Robinson 510
Wayne Cooper 425
Bob Gross 354
Sam Bowie 342
Lloyd Neal 324
Caldwell Jones 322

PERSONAL FOULS
Clyde Drexler 2,582
Jerome Kersey 2,465
Larry Steele 1,832
Kevin Duckworth 1,753
Mychal Thompson 1,696
Terry Porter 1,429
Bob Gross 1,415
Clifford Robinson 1,313
Buck Williams 1,285
Lloyd Neal 1,271

DISQUALIFICATIONS
Larry Steele 45
Tom Owens 37
Jerome Kersey 37
Clyde Drexler 32
Bob Gross 29
Kevin Duckworth 27
Mychal Thompson 25
Clifford Robinson 25
Steve Johnson 23
Kenny Carr 19

1971-72 PRESS BOOK

GEOFF PETRIE
Co-Rookie of 1970-71

PORTLAND TRAIL BLAZERS

TRAIL BLAZERS TEAM HIGHS

POINTS
Game:	156	vs. Denver (116), 11-22-83
	156	vs. LA Clippers (122), 2-1-86
Half:	86	vs. Golden State, 1-5-86
Quarter	49	vs. San Antonio (1st quarter), 11-25-90
	49	vs. Boston (4th quarter), 1-3-76
	49	at Denver (4th quarter), 2-13-81

FIELD GOALS
Game:	65	vs. Denver, 11-22-83
Half:	38	vs. Denver, 11-13-90
Quarter:	22	at Denver, 2-13-81
	22	vs. San Antonio, 11-25-90

FIELD GOALS ATTEMPTED
Game:	125	vs. Atlanta, 11-18-70
	125	at New York, 12-8-70
	125	vs. Atlanta, 2-4-71
Half:	69	at New York, 12-8-70
Quarter:	41	at LA Lakers, 12-6-70

FIELD GOAL PERCENTAGE
Game:	.697	vs. LA Clippers (62-89), 2-1-86

3-POINT FIELD GOALS MADE
Game:	12	at LA Clippers, 2-21-92
Half:	7	vs. Atlanta, 1-28-91
	7	vs. Orlando, 4-14-91

3-POINT FIELD GOALS ATTEMPTED
Game:	22	Golden State, 4-7-92
	22	at Atlanta (OT), 3-29-93
Half:	13	at Phoenix, 12-16-88

FREE THROWS MADE
Game:	53	vs. New York, 2-7-85
Half:	33	at Seattle, 3-27-91
Quarter:	22	at Seattle, 3-27-91

FREE THROWS ATTEMPTED
Game:	64	vs. New York, 2-7-85
Half:	41	vs. Seattle, 3-5-77
Quarter:	28	at New Orleans, 11-16-76

FREE THROW PERCENTAGE
Game:	1.000	at Indiana (30-30), 11-30-86

TOTAL REBOUNDS
Game:	75	vs. Cleveland (4 OT), 10-18-74
	71	vs. San Diego, 11-3-78
Half:	41	at Kansas City, 1-17-76
	41	vs. San Diego, 1-3-78
	41	vs. Utah, 2-5-82
Quarter:	26	vs. LA Lakers, 2-19-72

OFFENSIVE REBOUNDS
Game:	33	vs. New Orleans, 1-8-78

DEFENSIVE REBOUNDS
Game:	56	vs. Cleveland (4 OT), 10-18-74
	53	vs. Cleveland, 11-19-77

ASSISTS
Game:	49	vs. Denver, 11-13-90
Half:	29	vs. Denver, 11-13-90
Quarter:	18	vs. San Antonio, 11-25-90

PERSONAL FOULS
Game:	44	vs. Chicago (4 OT), 3-16-7
	42	at Atlanta, 1-16-77
Half:	27	at Atlanta, 1-16-77
Quarter:	18	at Atlanta, 1-16-77

DISQUALIFICATIONS
Game:	4	at Atlanta, 1-16-77
	4	at Indiana, 12-6-78
	4	vs. Denver, 11-13-88

STEALS
Game:	24	vs. Golden State, 3-17-84
Half:	15	vs. New Jersey, 11-24-89
Quarter:	9	vs. New Jersey, 11-24-89
	9	at San Antonio, 3-22-90

TURNOVERS
Game:	40	at Phoenix, 3-7-76
Half:	24	at Houston, 2-18-75

BLOCKED SHOTS
Game:	17	at New Orleans, 1-19-79
Half:	12	vs. Detroit, 1-6-80

FIVE HIGHEST SCORING GAMES
156-116	vs. Denver, 11-22-83
156-121	vs. LA Clippers, 2-1-86
155-129	vs. Denver, 11-13-90
155-156	vs. Chicago (4 OT), 3-16-84
150-113	vs. San Antonio, 1-9-77

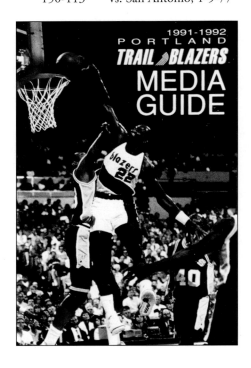

ALL-TIME TRAIL BLAZERS HONORS

PLAYERS

RON BREWER
NBA All-Rookie Team—1978-79.
SAM BOWIE
NBA All-Rookie Team—1984-85.
CLYDE DREXLER
All-NBA—1st team, 1991-92; 2nd team, 1987-88, 1990-91; 3rd team, 1989-90. All-Star Games—(8) 1986, 1988, 1889, 1990, 1991, 1992, 1993, 1994. Member, Gold Medal winning 1992 U.S. Olympic Team.
KEVIN DUCKWORTH
NBA Most Improved Player —1987-88. All-Star Games——(2) 1989, 1991.
BOB GROSS
NBA All-Defensive Team—2nd team, 1977-78.
LIONEL HOLLINS
NBA All-Rookie Team—1975-76. NBA All-Defensive Team—1st team, 1977-78; 2nd team, 1978-79. All-Star Game—(1) 1978.
STEVE JOHNSON
All-Star Game—(1) 1988.
MAURICE LUCAS
All-NBA—2nd team, 1977-78. NBA All-Defensive Team—1st team, 1977-78; 2nd team, 1978-79. All-Star Game—(3) 1977, 1978, 1979.
TRACY MURRAY
NBA 3-Point Field Goal Percentage Leader—1993-94 (.459).
CALVIN NATT
NBA All-Rookie Team—1979-80.
LLOYD NEAL
NBA All-Rookie Team—1972-73.
JIM PAXSON
All-NBA—2nd team, 1983-84. All-Star Games—(2) 1983, 1984.
GEOFF PETRIE
NBA Rookie of the Year—1970-71. NBA All-Rookie Team—1970-71. All-Star Games—(2) 1971, 1974.
TERRY PORTER
J. Walter Kennedy Citizenship Award—1992-93. All-Star Games—(2) 1991, 1993.

KELVIN RANSEY
NBA All-Rookie Team—1980-81.
CLIFFORD ROBINSON
NBA Sixth Man of the Year Award—1993. All-Star Game—(1) 1994.
LARRY STEELE
NBA Steals Leader—1973-74 (2.68 avg.).
MYCHAL THOMPSON
NBA All-Rookie Team—1978-79.
KIKI VANDEWEGHE
NBA 3-Point Field Goal Percentage Leader—1986-87 (.481).
BILL WALTON
NBA Most Valuable Player—1977-78. NBA Playoffs Most Valuable Player—1977-78. All-NBA—1st team, 1977-78; 2nd team, 1976-77. NBA All-Defensive team—1st team, 1976-77, 1977-78. All-Star Game—(2) 1977, 1978. NBA Rebound Leader—1976-77 (14.4 avg.) NBA Blocked Shots Leader—1976-77 (3.25 avg.).
KERMIT WASHINGTON
NBA All-Defensive Team—2nd team, 1979-80, 1980-81. All-Star Game—(1) 1980.
SIDNEY WICKS
NBA Rookie of the Year—1971-72. NBA All-Rookie Team—1971-72. All-Star Games—(4) 1972, 1973, 1974, 1975.
BUCK WILLIAMS
NBA All-Defensive Team—1st team, 1989-90, 1990-91; 2nd team 1991-92. NBA Field Goal Percentage Leader—1990-91 (.602), 1991-92 (.604)

COACHES & EXECUTIVES

RICK ADELMAN
1991 West All-Star Team Head Coach
BUCKY BUCKWALTER
1990-91 NBA Executive of the Year
JACK RAMSAY
1978 West All-Star Team Head Coach
MIKE SCHULER
1986-87 NBA Coach of the Year

INDIVIDUAL BLAZERS RECORDS

POINTS
Game: 51 .....Geoff Petrie, at Houston, 1-20-73
              51 .....Geoff Petrie, vs. Houston, 3-16-73
Season: 2,185 ....Clyde Drexler, 81 games, 1987-88
Average: 27.2 ....Clyde Drexler, 78 games, 1988-89

FIELD GOALS
Game: 20 .....Geoff Petrie, at Golden State, 2-8-73
              20 .....Geoff Petrie, at Philadelphia, 3-20-74
              20 .....Lionel Hollins, vs. Boston, 2-22-77
              20 .....Clyde Drexler, vs. New York, 1-22-89
Season: 849 ....Clyde Drexler, 81 games, 1987-88

FIELD GOALS ATTEMPTED
Game: 37 .....Geoff Petrie, at Golden State, 2-8-73
Season: 1,837 ....Sidney Wicks, 82 games, 1971-72

FIELD GOAL PERCENTAGE
Season: .612 ....Dave Twardzik (263-430), 1976-77

3-POINT FIELD GOALS MADE
Game: 7 ....Terry Porter, at Golden State, 11-14-92
               7 ....Terry Porter, at Utah, 1-2-93
Season: 143 ....Terry Porter, 81 games, 1992-93

3-POINT FIELD GOALS ATTEMPTED
Game   12 ....Terry Porter, at Atlanta (OT), 3-29-93
              10 ....Terry Porter, at LA Clippers, 2-21-92
              10 ....Clyde Drexler, at Milwaukee, 3-31-94
Season: 345 ....Terry Porter, 81 games, 1992-93

3-POINT FIELD GOAL PERCENTAGE
Game: 1.000 ....Terry Porter (7-7), at Golden St., 11-14-92
Season: .459 ....Tracy Murray (50-109), 1993-94

FREE THROWS MADE
Game: 18 ....Geoff Petrie, vs. Seattle, 3-19-71
              18 ....Kiki Vandeweghe, vs. Seattle, 3-21-86
Season: 523 ....Kiki Vandeweghe, 79 games, 1985-86

FREE THROWS ATTEMPTED
Game: 22 ....Calvin Natt, at Detroit, 2-23-80
              22 ....Kiki Vandeweghe, vs. Seattle, 3-21-86
Season: 621 ....Sidney Wicks, 82 games, 1971-72

FREE THROW PERCENTAGE
Game: 1.000 ....Jim Barnett (16-16), vs. Atlanta, 11-18-70
Season: .896 ....Kiki Vandeweghe (369-412), 1984-85

TOTAL REBOUNDS
Game: 27 .....Sidney Wicks (2 OT), at LA Lakers, 2-26-75
              26 ....LeRoy Ellis, vs. Buffalo, 10-27-70
              26 ....Bill Walton, at Golden State, 12-30-77
Season: 967 ....Lloyd Neal, 82 games, 1972-73
Average: 14.4 ....Bill Walton, 65 games, 1976-77

OFFENSIVE REBOUNDS
Game: 11 .....Sidney Wicks (2 OT), at LA Lakers, 2-26-75
              11 ....Sam Bowie (OT), at LA Lakers, 4-7-85
              11 ....John Johnson, vs. Atlanta, 11-14-74
              11 ....Steve Hawes, vs. Golden State, 12-21-75
              11 ....Kermit Washington, vs. Milwaukee, 3-18-80
Season: 325 ....Kermit Washington, 80 games, 1979-80
Average: 4.1 ....Kermit Washington, 80 games, 1979-80

DEFENSIVE REBOUNDS
Game: 22 ....Bill Walton (OT), at Golden State, 1-24-76
              20 ....Bill Walton, vs. Golden State, 10-25-74
              20 ....Bill Walton, vs. Washington, 1-27-76
              20 ....Bill Walton, at Golden State, 12-30-77
Season: 723 ....Bill Walton, 65 games, 1976-77
Average: 11.2 ....Bill Walton, 58 games, 1977-78

ASSISTS
Game: 20 ....Rod Strickland, vs. Phoenix, 4-5-94
Season: 831 ....Terry Porter, 82 games, 1987-88
Average: 10.1 ....Terry Porter, 82 games, 1987-88

STEALS
Game: 10 ....Larry Steele, vs. LA Lakers 11-16-74
              10 ....Clyde Drexler, at Milwaukee, 1-10-86
Season: 217 ....Larry Steele, 81 games, 1973-74
Average: 2.7 ....Larry Steele, 81 games, 1973-74
          2.7 ....Clyde Drexler, 78 games, 1988-89

PERSONAL FOULS
Season: 340 ....Steve Johnson, 79 games, 1986-87
Average: 4.3 ....Steve Johnson, 79 games, 1986-87

BLOCKED SHOTS
Game: 9 ....Bill Walton, at Golden State, 10-22-74
               9 ....Bill Walton, at Denver, 1-26-77
               9 ....Mychal Thompson (OT), at N.J., 2-20-81
Season: 211 ....Bill Walton, 65 games, 1976-77
Average: 3.2 ....Bill Walton, 65 games, 1976-77

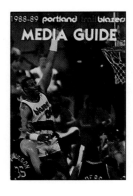

POINTS
Game: 43 .....Clyde Drexler (OT), at LA Lakers, 4-29-92
       41 .....Terry Porter, vs. Utah, 5-19-92

FIELD GOALS
Game: 16 .....Billy Ray Bates, vs. Kansas City, 4-5-81

FIELD GOALS ATTEMPTED
Game: 30 .....Clyde Drexler, at Phoenix, 5-9-92

3-POINT FIELD GOALS MADE
Game: 6 .....Terry Porter, vs. Utah, 5-16-92

3-POINT FIELD GOALS ATTEMPTED
Game   9 .....Terry Porter (2 OT) vs. San Antonio, 5-15-90
        9 .....Terry Porter (OT), vs. San Antonio, 5-19-90
        9 .....Terry Porter, at Detroit, 6-14-90

FREE THROWS MADE
Game: 15 .....Darnell Valentine, at Phoenix, 4-22-84
       15 .....Terry Porter, vs. Dallas, 4-26-90
       15 .....Terry Porter (OT), vs. Detroit, 6-7-90

FREE THROWS ATTEMPTED
Game: 17 .....Calvin Natt, vs. Seattle, 4-22-83

FREE THROW PERCENTAGE
Game: 1.000 .....Terry Porter (OT) (15-15), at Detroit, 6-7-90

TOTAL REBOUNDS
Game: 24 .....Bill Walton, at Philadelphia, 6-3-77

OFFENSIVE REBOUNDS
Game: 10 .....Tom Owens, at Seattle, 4-6-80

DEFENSIVE REBOUNDS
Game: 20 .....Bill Walton, at Philadelphia, 6-3-77
       20 .....Bill Walton, vs. Philadelphia, 6-5-77

ASSISTS
Game: 15 .....Darnell Valentine, at LA Lakers, 4-26-83
       15 .....Terry Porter, vs. Houston, 4-26-87
       15 .....Clyde Drexler, vs. Utah, 5-9-91
       15 .....Rod Strickland, vs. Houston, 5-3-94

STEALS
Game: 8 .....Lionel Hollins, at LA Lakers, 5-8-77

BLOCKED SHOTS
Game: 8 .....Bill Walton, vs. Philadelphia, 6-5-77

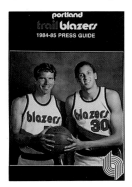

HEAD COACHES

Rolland Todd
1970-71

Stu Inman
1971-72

Jack McCloskey
1972-74

Lenny Wilkens
1974-76

Jack Ramsay
1976-86

Mike Schuler
1986-89

Rick Adelman
1989-94

P.J. Carlesimo
1994-

TRAINERS

Leo Marty
1970-74

Ron Culp
1974-84

Mike Shimensky
1984-94

Jay Jensen
1994-